DRESSAGE
in the
FOURTH DIMENSION

DRESSAGE
in the
FOURTH
DIMENSION

SHERRY ACKERMAN, PhD

Foreword by Linda Kohanov

Second Edition

NEW WORLD LIBRARY
NOVATO, CALIFORNIA

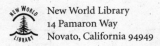

New World Library
14 Pamaron Way
Novato, California 94949

A previous version of this book was published in 1997 by Xenophon Press.

Text design by Tracy Pitts

Ackerman, Sherry L.
Dressage in the fourth dimension / Sherry Ackerman ; foreword by
Linda Kohanov. — 2nd ed.
      p.   cm.
Includes bibliographical references and index.
ISBN 978-1-57731-623-7 (hardcover : alk. paper)
1. Dressage. 2. Horsemanship. I. Title.
SF309.5.A25 2008
798.2'3—dc22   2008030806

First printing, November 2008
ISBN 978-1-57731-623-7
Printed in Canada on 100% postconsumer-waste recycled paper

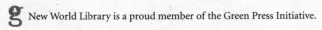

New World Library is a proud member of the Green Press Initiative.

10 9 8 7 6 5 4 3 2 1

To the growing community of people who recognize the role of animal spirituality in the evolution of consciousness; to those who see the philosophia perennis *in everyday life; and to those who are forging an integral worldview, fully aware that all life matters*

IN GRATEFUL MEMORY OF
DR. PAULOS MAR GREGORIOS

CONTENTS

FOREWORD

The book you hold in your hand represents an incredible act of courage and vision. In 1997, when *Dressage in the Fourth Dimension* was originally published, bestsellers like Susan Chernak McElroy's *Animals as Teachers and Healers* and Monty Roberts's *The Man Who Listens to Horses* were a couple of years away from becoming bestsellers.

At that time, those of us who did, in fact, see horses as sentient beings, and even as teachers and healers, kept quiet about it for the most part. To say that you were riding for any reason other than sport or recreation was suspect. The phrase "horse lover" was applied with disdain. And anyone who admitted to having a spiritual experience in the presence of one of these amazing creatures was considered eccentric at best and more than likely delusional.

Along came Sherry Ackerman, an accomplished equestrian and philosopher who not only suggested that riding can be used as a path of transformation but also all but guaranteed that anyone who learns to ride well *can't help* but be transformed. In this book, she discusses dressage — an ancient tradition originally developed to train war horses — as a martial art. As in karate and aikido, students who go through this rigorous training develop heightened physical, emotional, mental, and spiritual awareness. Yet unlike every other martial art in existence, dressage demands that you access this expanded level of consciousness, poise, courage, and balance through an intimate, cooperative relationship with another being — and a powerful, nonpredatory being at that.

Learning to harmonize with a horse, Ackerman reveals, is what she calls a yoga-of-two, which leads to a palpable experience of oneness. The sophisticated discipline of dressage attracts people with a desire to excel, to compete, to win. And it is the ultimate trick of the divine that — as the author so eloquently demonstrates throughout this now classic book — the reflection, exploration, and self-knowledge required eventually catapult truly serious riders out of their egos and into a state of union with not only their horses but also a deeper, mystical reality, a "fourth dimension of the spirit."

Great nonfiction writers uncover the poetry in everyday life. Ackerman's prose is both graceful and dense, offering in each concentrated chapter not just one or two quotable gems but several dozen worthy of posting at the barn or recording in your journal, quotes that will inspire hours of contemplation and conversation.

Even if you never intend to ride at this level, or ride at all, you will recognize that the observations and advice in *Dressage in the Fourth Dimension* apply to the horse-human relationship as it evolves in the twenty-first century. Even if you don't own a horse, the insights contained in this modern treatise on mutual interspecies transformation offer much food for thought. It is ironic that, for thousands of years, these sensitive yet powerful beings carried human bodies around the world, allowing us to explore terrain we would have struggled to traverse on foot. Yet even as they've been released from their roles as beasts of burden, horses have not become obsolete. They stand

beckoning at the edge of a new wilderness — the land-
scape of consciousness itself — waiting for us to ac-
cept the challenge to live life to its fullest potential.
Sherry Ackerman offers us one of the first and most
potent road maps for the journey these animals are
ready, willing, and able to help us undertake.

Linda Kohanov,
author of *The Tao of Equus*

PREFACE

"Write what you need to know." This advice, given to me years ago by a wise mentor, is what I've tried to do throughout my equestrian and academic careers. Writing is a solitary endeavor, and although I enjoy the retreat and silence while capturing ideas in words, *Dressage in the Fourth Dimension* taught me that everything I write is essentially a collaborative process. Sometimes the words were the result of giving voice to a soul on fire. Other times, there was only the silence of soulful ambiguity. In this visit to the fourth dimension, I experienced myself as a fluid being with shadowy boundaries, constantly flowing between soulful silence and collaboration, into and through others, always dynamic, always in a mutual dance.

This book is a product of the realization that my *two* lives are, in fact, *one* life. While it appears that I wear both the hat of a dressage clinician and that of a philosophy professor, it has gradually become clear to me that these are the same hat. As my interest in philosophy has deepened, I've become increasingly intrigued by philosophy's relationship to art, especially the *art de vivre*. Specifically, I've wondered if an individual's experience of the beautiful constituted gnosis — direct experience of the supernatural or divine — and if so, did it have the potential to be life transforming?

Horses summon our instinctual, primal selves and evoke our subjectivity. Astride them, as mythical centaurs, we reconnect with unconscious memories that have been buried away or safely girdled up, and these memories begin circulating in our psyches. We look at our horses and see the immanent incarnation of powerful forces bottled up within us that we wish we had the courage to acknowledge. These shadow forces, when acknowledged, can make manifest our dreams and facilitate our actualization. Denied, they can destroy us. When these hidden feelings are agitated, we are challenged by the options they offer us.

C.J. Jung pointed us to life's paradoxes, and he left instructions telling us that it's important to embrace seeming contradictions as we travel the never-ending journey toward becoming fully human. Horses, with the ability to either liberate us or hurt us, personify these paradoxes. Archetypically, the horse is not autonomous. It appears to represent different forces. Which one it represents depends on our individual phase of development: the horse can act in the place of the child, the anima or animus, the great mother or great father, or the wise old woman or wise old man. The archetype carries meaning according to each individual's actual level of personal maturity.

We are living in radical times, poised on the edge of a new paradigm. The lure of materialism is losing its potency as people awaken to the limitlessness of consciousness. When we bring this awareness to the art of dressage, we are confronted with our own shortcomings. We stand face to face with our personal demons. This is the dressage crisis. We can stick our heads in the sand and ignore it, or we can press on — we can take the long, intense journey to a place where ego is extinguished. This is not a place marked by *knowing about*, but one in which we *know*. Although it's ineffable, we recognize it when we arrive. We become humble in this reverent place.

I hope this book changes how you see the relationships between art, through the lens of dressage; nature, through the lens of the horse; and yourself. This exploration has been for me so sacrosanct that I've had difficulty working within the confines of written language: words seem grievously inadequate to describe the liberation I've discovered on the path of self-realization through dressage. Although a slim volume, *Fourth Dimension* is a weighty book and should be read slowly and contemplatively. I've considered the idea that it might be best to read the final chapter first, as the story truly begins where it ends. And although, in an absolute sense, the book was written from the backs of my horses, you don't need to know anything about horses or dressage to read it. It is really a primer on mysticism. For some, the vehicle to self-realization may be psychedelics, meditation, or martial arts, but for me it was dressage. It doesn't matter which vehicle is used. A person doesn't return unchanged from direct experience of the One.

My own journey spanned thirty years and at times involved such philosophical upheaval that my personal life stood on the shores of chaos. For me, the crisis is over but the journey continues. I embrace all of life's experiences, aware of my potential for simultaneous immanence and transcendence. I no longer simply look *in at* dressage but also look *out from it*.

The subject and the object have merged, and nothing about my human existence can ever be the same again.

A decade ago, *Fourth Dimension* acknowledged my particular point of view. I wrote what I needed to know, at that time, for my particular level of maturity. Ten years have deepened those insights, amplified my understanding, and crystallized my vision. And still, what I have written here is what I need to know. In the same way that the archetype of the horse is not autonomous, neither am I. In fully honoring my collaboration with the horses, the geometry, the motion, and the ideas, I find that the fourth dimension has become a space that I can more naturally, and authentically, inhabit.

INTRODUCTION

*It is time to throw off the shackles, to reclaim that which
every child knows and is taught to forget: the
essential right to create without interference or shame.*

— **MICHELE CASSOU AND STEWART CUBLEY,**
*Life, Paint, and Passion: Reclaiming the
Magic of Spontaneous Expression*

Very simply, this is a book about the art of dressage. It is not about technique, but about essence, the fundamental nature of the art. It's also a book about philosophy, for without philosophy there is no art. There may be craft or technique, but there is no art.

Art is the bride of philosophy. It is philosophy's feminine side safeguarding the knowledge quest from the tyranny of hard, data-driven, objective analysis. Art constitutes a legitimate way-of-knowing that is beginning to be recognized by those who discern a new paradigm: a paradigm of inclusiveness, integration, and integrity. A paradigm that makes a global community possible. A paradigm that is not patriarchal. Art, as differentiated from craft or technique, is a vehicle through which an individual may experience the beautiful. This experience involves an awareness of the unity of all things — of interconnectedness, of oneness. Awareness of unitary reality expands consciousness and facilitates human perception of the immaterial realms.

When an individual knows oneness, as opposed to knowing about oneness, she or he is necessarily transformed. This is gnosis, and it's impossible to return from this experience unchanged. Once begun, the transformative process takes on a life of its own in which being and knowledge act reciprocally. Whereas transformation was originally initiated by knowledge, now knowledge is initiated by transformation. As Aldous Huxley has observed, "Knowledge is a function of being. When there is a change in the being of the knower, there is a corresponding change in the nature and amount of knowing."[1] In the pages that follow, I have used parable and anecdote, allegory and paradox, to advance the idea that dressage offers a powerful vehicle for experiencing unity consciousness and subsequent transformation.

A doctrine of the unity of reality is referred to as the *philosophia perennis,* a term coined by Gottfried Leibniz. The *philosophia perennis* is immemorial and universal. Like a perennial wildflower, it is hardy and prolific and, as Huxley says, can therefore be "found among the traditionary lore of primitive peoples in every region of the world, and in its fully developed forms it has a place in every one of the higher religions."[2] Huxley offers an overview of the perennial philosophy in his classic *The Perennial Philosophy:*

> *The metaphysic that recognizes a Divine Reality substantial to the world of things and lives and minds; the psychology that finds in the soul something similar to, even identical with, Divine Reality, and the ethic that places man's final end in the knowledge of the immanent and transcendent Ground of all being.*[3]

Although we are the many participating in the one, we are not directly or immediately conscious of this relationship until certain conceptual patterns in our psyches have been set in motion.

Dressage, as pure aesthetic expression, is a journey on which one has an opportunity to awaken to the consciousness of participation in the unity of reality.

It gives us a way to get beyond mere secondhand discussion of the subject matter and move toward a firsthand experience of the perennial philosophy. Cassou and Cubley tell us that "the process of any aesthetic activity... — not the product, but the process" — is a doorway into a direct experience of the essential life force.[4] Existing art paradigms have become too concerned with the final fruit of the creative experience, erroneously equating aesthetics with aesthetics' results, thereby requiring analytic justification. This, in dressage, is manifest as an obsession with competition and constitutes an obvious barrier to one's openness to new perceptions.

The basic tenet of this book is that the aesthetic process, irrespective of product, is the critical factor in one's experience of the beautiful. A hidden wave of "passion lies just below the surface of most people's lives," say Cassou and Cubley, "a passion yearning to be liberated from the paralyzing myths of talent, skill, inspiration, accomplishment, success and failure."[5] The aesthetic process allows this passion to speak. In this book, I ask you to view dressage as an art that stimulates your sense of aliveness, energy, and vulnerability. The actual dressage ride is just the echo of a much deeper process. What is reflected in motion, rhythm, and balance are the outer garments of a journey taking place in the inner manège — that is, the "inner riding school." The real movements have been created in the manège of the psyche, or as Cassou and Cubley put it, "The true artistic product is the personal transformation that has taken place within the ... experience itself."[6]

The book begins, as the final chapter concludes, with the call to awaken to the moment — to become present and to experience the unity of all creation. Chapter 1 introduces sacred geometry as an ancient art capable of revealing the nature of our relationship to the cosmos. This chapter suggests that the unconscious self is led to contemplate universal spiritual laws as it participates in the moving mandalas that are the figures of the manège. Chapters 2 and 3 use the dressage training pyramid as a metaphor for exploring deeper metaphysical insights. These chapters discuss the reciprocity of relationship and the raw experience of primal energies, and they show that these are tools for liberation from the ego. Transcendental union and responsible power, often considered mutually exclusive, are instead compatible elements of the mystic's journey. Immanence and transcendence, embodied in the horse, form an integrated, nondual process.

Chapter 4 focuses on the coveted dressage qualities of balance, harmony, and freedom as aspects of gnosis.

The chapter title, "The Hymn of Love," harks back to the Orphic Hymns, a set of preclassical poetic compositions recited in ancient mystery rites and purification rituals. This chapter positions love as self-transcendence, the very motor of spiritual development. "The Hymn of Love" sets the stage for chapter 5, which details the path of the soul from its seemingly material captivity in mortality, back to the infinite, immortal freedom of the One. Through the imagery of alchemy, this chapter describes the purification of the soul as it endures the dark night that gives way to the light.

Like an *ouroboros* — the symbol of a snake eternally eating its own tail — the book ends, in chapter 6, where it started. The call to awaken, become present, and experience gnosis is seen as the gate to the fourth dimension. Unity consciousness, whether it's what Eckhart Tolle calls "consciousness," Jill Bolte Taylor calls the "right brain," or what I identify as the "fourth dimension," is what humankind separated from, and what we are again — one by one, each in his or her own time — reuniting with.

CHAPTER 1

SACRED GEOMETRY

The Figures of the Manège

Philosophy is written in this grand book — I mean the universe — which stands continually open to our gaze, but it cannot be understood unless one first learns to comprehend the language and interpret the characters in which it is written. It is written in the language of mathematics, and its characters are triangles, circles and other geometrical figures, without which it is humanly impossible to understand a single word of it; without these, one is wandering about in a dark labyrinth.

— **GALILEO GALILEI,**
Il Saggiatore (The Assayer), 1623

The earliest reference to dressage is found in the writings of the Greek historian and philosophical essayist Xenophon. Born in Athens around 430 BCE, Xenophon belonged to an equestrian family in the deme of Erchia. Early in his life, he had come under the influence of Socrates and had received schooling in classical geometry. Xenophon's education led him to view geometry and numbers as components of the simplest and most essential philosophical language.

Geometry, as performed by the ancient Greeks, was the study of spatial order through the measure and relationships of forms. The geometer allowed his or her mind to become a channel though which the physical, immanent earth could receive the abstract, transcendent life of the heavens. In geometry, the cosmological dualisms were resolved. Geometric practice provided an approach to comprehending both the order of the universe and that which can be sustained in it. The contemplation of figures as still moments revealed continuous, timeless, universal truths generally hidden from sensory perception.

The Greeks viewed participation in geometric activity as an avenue for intellectual and spiritual insight.[1] This view was fundamental to dressage. The ancient teachings held that beauty was expressed by harmony, which was born of perfect balance. The body, mind, and spirit of the rider were to attain an integrated state of balance. The development of any one component at the expense of the other two would result in disharmony and discord. When equally attended to, the three components produced a harmonious partnership between horse and rider, which expressed itself in beauty.[2]

Seen from an archetypal level, "geometry" and "number" described basic, causal energies in their interwoven, eternal dance. To be immersed in a geometric diagram was to enter into a kind of philosophic contemplation. Ancient Greek teachings held that humans had the intellectual capacity to recognize patterns in space, comprehend part-whole relationships, perceive opposites in simultaneity, and grasp functions that appeared irrational from an analytic standpoint. This constituted the first confrontation between the philosophical principles of dressage and the intellect and/or rationality. The figures of the manège — that is, the circle, square, and other geometric figures that horse and rider trace while training in order to develop balance, rhythm, and other skills — when carefully executed by both horse and rider, provide an opportunity for a merging of the physical, mental, and spiritual dimensions.

All movement begins with its antithesis, immobility. The dot, in ancient cosmologies, represented universal consciousness — the source of all things, and the dwelling of the Spirit or the Not-Self. In the three-dimensional theater of dressage, we participate in the dot through the fully engaged halt. We sit, perfectly motionless in poised collection, with the horse's weight squarely distributed under our own supple position. In this immobility, time stands still. The halt is the eternal now, where past, present, and future are all one. We experience a lightness that enhances our sensitivity to the horse's balance. We sense our mount's almost imperceptible weight shifts through our own passive bodies. We experience the humility of the Not-Self as we realize that the halt, in immobility, contains the energy of every movement. The horse is catlike, ready to spring from soft-jointed hindquarters through its coiled loins. As long as we do not disturb the collection, the horse remains prepared — powerfully positioned — for instantaneous movement in any direction, at any gait. We are no longer merely astride the horse. We sit in a stream of consciousness: the motion of immobility.

In its first manifestation, the dot elongates to form the line, the symbol of universal intelligence (which derives from universal consciousness). Accordingly, the halt extends into the work the horse and rider do while tracing straight lines and becomes the motion of truth. On these lines, the horse finds the longitudinal balance necessary to develop free, pure gaits. Impulsion is expressed as the horse thrusts powerfully forward and upward. The ideas of free, forward, calm, and straight find a workplace — that is, they become practical considerations — as the movement becomes a dance in which horse and rider think the same thought. The aids — the signals or cues that the rider gives the horse to indicate that it's time to execute certain movements or gaits — become invisible as the dancers mutually participate in universal intelligence. A harmony grows between horse and rider in which neither partner is consumed by the other. Rhythm, relaxation, and contact lose their quantitative value and, instead, become aesthetic tools. At this point, dressage renounces any association with sport and assumes its rightful place among the arts.

The circle, so central to dressage, represents the form established in the material sphere by these other superphysical activities. It is the bent line, the curved elongated dot. The Greek mathematician and philosopher Pythagoras (c. 570 BCE) observed that each one of the primary numbers is a qualitative, archetypal essence possessing a distinct, living personality.[3] This personality makes itself known to us as we participate in the manifestations of these principles through the figures of the manège. Pythagoras used the circle to represent the monad — the ultimate, indivisible unit — as the instrument of truth, the not-many, the male-female, the invulnerable destiny, happiness, blending, harmony, and order. The monad serves as a foundation for existence, because within it resides the raw potentiality for everything that *is*. It is the beginning, middle, and end of all things. Since the monad is viewed as pure light, as being sunlike and authoritative, without it there is neither composition nor knowledge of anything.[4]

The circle, a school for the lateral balance, provides a place where the physical instruments of both horse and rider become equally strengthened and suppled from side to side. It is here that equine and human weaknesses and disparities in physical development awkwardly present themselves. More often than not, the rider responds to the horse's underdeveloped hindquarters with his or her overdeveloped legs, hands, and back, generating a physical antagonism by blaming or by limiting the horse (blocking the horse in such a way that the horse's full gymnastic potential becomes limited), or even by employing militant gymnastic techniques. The humble rider, however, takes a different path and works toward resolution by taking responsibility for blending with the horse. When the rider recognizes his or her own imperfections and intolerances, corrections naturally follow. These true

dresseurs, not the *dompteurs* (trainers who lack fi-
nesse), experience the growth of virtue.

Ennobling character changes follow. The rider's
attention span lengthens, endurance increases, and
tolerance of pain and discomfort increases. The rider
becomes braver, and stronger in body, mind, and
spirit. His or her powers of concentration deepen to a
meditative state, and he or she becomes oblivious to
anything outside the harmonious absorption of com-
munion with the horse. The rider's focus sharpens and
then cuts the irrelevant details away, making the rider
steadfast in body, mind, and spirit. Wiser in analysis,
more resourceful in synthesis, the rider finds his or her
task and does it with dispatch. With profound empa-
thy born of love for the horse, tempered by respect,
and urged on by a growing tolerance, the rider becomes
master of the horse, but with enough humility not
to displease the horse.[5] Nowhere is the body-mind
relationship more sharply evident than in the circle,
the workshop of the lateral field of balance. Too many
riders focus on the circle only as it affects the horse and
fail to consider the part it plays in their own experience.

In 1981, the neuropsychologist and neurobiologist
Roger Sperry won the Nobel Prize for his pioneering

work on the differences between the left and right sides, or hemispheres, of the brain. His research indicates that each of us is naturally predisposed toward either right- or left-hemisphere dominance. Yielding to this innate predisposition ipso facto limits consciousness. Just as blind acceptance of analytic, technically oriented paradigms — in exclusive pursuit of hard, cold, objective knowledge — rob human life of its warmth, of its beauty and subjective meaning, so do single-minded subjective perspectives lack sufficient clarity and definition. These imbalanced perspectives fail to affirm the importance of human values and experience and ignore our need for comfort, solace, and purpose.

Today polarity is a central tenet in both science and psychology. The initial energy of the universe polarizes into myriad forms, but when the duality disappears — as it must — only one reality remains. In our physical brains, this polarity can be seen in the left and right hemispheres. Synchronizing these two sides is a fundamental goal of consciousness expansion and of meditation in all its forms.[6]

Sperry's research paved the way for a more integrated model of consciousness by providing clear evidence that the corpus callosum, the huge bundle of nerve fibers spanning the two hemispheres of the brain, could transmit knowledge from one hemisphere to the other, indicating that synchronized hemispheric activity was neurologically possible.[7]

The correctly ridden dressage circle trains our nervous systems to permit synchronized hemispheric activity. In all of us, body movement and functions on the left side of the body are controlled by the right brain hemisphere and, conversely, the right side of the body is controlled by the left hemisphere. When riders are physically imbalanced — for example, in favor of the right side — we can be certain that left-brain hemispheric activity in these riders is overpowering the efforts of the right hemisphere. They are enslaved by analysis and empirical observation. They lack a sense of artistry and ride like technicians. On the other hand, right-hemisphere-dominant riders, with more command over and coordination on the left sides of their physical bodies, invariably offer brilliance and panache, though often at the expense of accuracy and correct gymnastics. The ideal, of course, is to blend artistry with technical skill.

About three years ago, I accepted an aspiring dressage rider as a serious student. Bonnie was tall, lean, and physically fit. She was intelligent, and her emotional and psychological houses were in order. After watching her ride a few times, I asked her if she liked to draw or paint. She replied that she had enjoyed making art earlier in her life, but that it had been crowded out by the press of adult life. Her right leg, seat, back, and hand were coordinated and strong, while her left side struggled for even a modicum of control. I make a practice of playing music of the Italian Renaissance in my arena, and during Bonnie's lessons I would occasionally ask her if she recognized a given composer. Over time, she shared that she had once been very involved with music and had even been an accomplished trumpeter, but that she had not remained interested in recent years. I tucked this information away and worked single-mindedly toward helping her find balance between the two sides of her body.

After about a year and a half, Bonnie's circles to the left began to be as good as her circles to the right. She was becoming more symmetrical. I continued to work quietly, "chopping wood and carrying water," as the ancient Zen parable directs, until one day Bonnie presented me with a carefully wrapped gift of her own artwork. Within a few months after that initial presentation, she shared with me that she had been searching through a musical archive with the goal of eventually

choreographing a musical freestyle dressage performance (a "Kur") for herself and her horse. As Bonnie's
physical body became balanced, her brain hemispheric
synchronization became neurologically facilitated. Liberated from left-brain dominance, she was discovering
more integrated ways of knowing. Only a few months
after this breakthrough, this former technician crossed
the threshold, via the circle, into equestrian art.

The universality of the monad can be seen in yet
another physical context. In 1714, the German philosopher and mathematician Gottfried Wilhelm Leibniz
wrote that "reality cannot be found except in One single
source, because of the interconnection of all things
with one another."[8] During Leibniz's lifetime, this sort
of metaphysical system was either rejected as unverifi-
able or interpreted as proof of the existence of God.
Modern physics, however, has begun to supply evidence
that the entire material universe may, in fact, be composed of wave functions. According to this theory,
matter consists of interconnected wave structures, all
emanating from one unified source, thus giving credence to the conceptual monad. Not only are all things
interconnected, but they also participate in a reality that
transcends their material appearance. Waves are pure,
temporal patterns, dynamic configurations composed

of amplitude, interval, and frequency. According to wave theory, every living body, as well as all elemental or inanimate objects, are composed of waves that vibrate at the molecular level. Some philosophers speak of reaching a state of consciousness in which one is constantly aware of the integration between the apparent external vibratory field, which manifests objectively as matter, and the inner subjective field, which is a unified, or monadic, state of consciousness.

Sri Aurobindo (1872–1950), an Indian political and spiritual leader, referred to this mode of perceptual awareness as "knowledge by identity" and regarded it as an important state in the process of spiritual development.[9] As we interact with external stimuli, we become aware that the continual flow of our internal faculties of perception and cognition directs our consciousness. The objective world intertwines with the entire physical, mental, and psychological condition of the perceiving individual and, consequently, is altered by changes in his or her inward condition.[10] This concept has serious implications for dressage riding.

The best dressage artists are individuals whose physical, mental, and psychological states are stable and positive. These people perceive their horses as capable, themselves as worthy, and the process as a flowing, forward continuum. They are neither angry nor impetuous. They don't blame their horses for their shortcomings, nor do they impose unrealistic demands on the horses' performances. Their spiritual eyes are open, and they appreciate the progress they are making in their dressage dance.

The visualizations of such dressage artists are harmonious, empathetic, light, and fluid. Consequently, it comes as no surprise when their horses read these riders' subjective states and then fulfill their expectations. Several years ago, I began working with a student who was intensely earnest about wanting to ride in the classical tradition. Sharon's zeal and commitment ran deep — so deep she couldn't find satisfaction in the slow, incremental progress that is the hallmark of dressage. A particular violence accompanied her need for finality, and perfectionism deprived her of her compassionate qualities. I struggled to help her see dressage as an ongoing and endless journey that demands no finished product, a discipline whose ends are never more important than the means.

This concept was not familiar to this tough-minded, goal-oriented taskmaster. The more furiously Sharon worked, the more resistance her horse displayed, and Sharon circled in a downward spiral of impatience

and fury. One day, amid the trauma, her horse softened under her and tried to show her the way. I seized
the moment and instructed her to reward the horse
immediately by stroking his neck, which Sharon flatly
refused to do. I was aghast and implored her to tell me
why she could not make a compassionate gesture in
response to the horse's willingness. Her reply was that
she didn't need to *stroke him*, as he knew he'd done
right by virtue of her not *striking him*! Hence, the only
reward this animal could expect was the avoidance of
punishment.

The flow of Sharon's internal faculties of perception and cognition, segregated from any awareness of
the horse himself, was directing her consciousness,
and this deeply vexed me. It took years for Sharon to
overcome her rigidly quantitative standards and unrealistic expectations. Finally, she began to trust Captain
Beudant's maxim, "Ask for much, be content with little, and reward often."[11] As she changed her inner perceptions and began to project positive images, love
and cooperation began to develop between herself and
her equine partner. Concomitantly, she experienced
personal growth in other areas of her life, developing a
more integrated outlook.

Completely relinquishing control of our internal
faculties of perception and cognition, and opening

ourselves to connecting with universal consciousness, can facilitate a state of expanded awareness. In order to make possible this kind of experience, we must be vulnerable and give up any control agenda. This principle is primary in Taoist philosophy. The *Tao Te Ching* advises:

In the pursuit of knowledge,
every day something is added.
In the practice of Tao,
every day something is dropped.
Less and less do you need to force things,
until finally you arrive at non-action.
When nothing is done,
nothing is left undone.
True mastery can be gained
by letting things go their own way.
It can't be gained by interfering.[12]

This state of expanded consciousness can't be gained by willing it. Only in the absence of the conscious will can a master dressage artist enter a state of awareness in which the right physical movement takes place by itself. Dressage rides the dressage. Nothing is done, because the rider has vanished into the ride; the fuel has been completely transformed into the flame. We are able to relinquish control in this manner when we trust the universal consciousness. The *ecuyer* (riding master) becomes adept in dressage not by conquering it but by becoming it.

I have personally experienced standing in the center of the small sand rectangle that constitutes the dressage arena, purposefully suspending cognition, and suddenly becoming aware of having heightened consciousness. While guiding a student toward a given principle of dressage, I discover that I am speaking beyond my knowledge, becoming a disciple of myself. I find new meanings in my own words and become aware that my mortal mind is being moved by an immortal agent. By an indefinable circumstance, I discover that I am just a mouthpiece for the wisdom of the ages. "Teaching" ceases to be a verb. I am faced with the realization that I cannot teach anyone anything, that my role is to give my students nothing, so that they can own their experience. My function is only to destroy the bindings attached to the artistic process, to destroy their beliefs about what they cannot do. As Michele Cassou has said, "I want to make them see that all they need is already inside them, like the water in a well that never runs dry."[13] I become an un-teacher. My students are students of themselves; the real teacher is the dressage process.

When we work from a state of consciousness in which we're aware of the integration — the resonance — between external vibratory fields and our own inner fields of perception, we reclaim our primal nature. We become a mantra understood by our horses. Language, as we know it, becomes secondary; the vibration of sound assumes primacy. We communicate by identity.

In ancient sacred geometry, the dyad was likened to courage, daring, and impulse because it was the first part of the monad to have separated from the whole.[14] The ancient Greeks also called the dyad by other titles — movement, relativity, and the ratio in proportionality — for the relation of two numbers takes every conceivable form. So, every thing, including the universe as a whole, is as One because of the natural and constitutive monad in each thing: but again, all is divisible because it necessarily partakes of the material dyad as well.[15] The dyad in dressage is the figure eight. In it, every property of the monad is experienced in the carefully ridden circle and then opposed in its own mirror image. If we look at this from the perspective of Taoist philosophy, we recognize in the dyad the yin and the yang. The resolution of this polarity fortifies dressage, because, in it, strength (yang) and suppleness (yin) are blended together.

The dyad prepares us for the triad, which we experience while riding in the serpentine figure. The triad shows us proportion, knowledge, and friendship. As we bend from right to left with every other turn, we learn about the kinetic properties of balance. Our dressage becomes dynamic, infused with enthusiasm. When this gestalt washes over our body and mind, we become physically and mentally supple. Any refusal on our part to yield control of our body and mind shows itself in the horse's stiff, clumsy negotiation of the turns. This is not a bad horse: this is a resistant rider.

The tetrad is the sacred square. The square is also one of the dressage figures traced by the horse and rider, and *tetrad* refers to the properties of the square in sacred geometry. When, in dressage, we participate in the tetrad — the square — we acknowledge the nature of change and justice. We experience the fractal dimension of geometry because everything in the universe, whatever its nature, turns out to be completed in the natural progression.[16] The tetrad was esteemed by Pythagoras as the most sacred number because it emanated from the "three in one," the first manifested unit. In ancient Greek arithmetic, the tetrad likewise represented a stage of completion, since the first four numbers make a sum of ten, which was believed to be

24

the very nature of number. Geometrically, the tetrad is expressed by the square. Metaphysically, the tetrad represents the four primary elements. Of all the solids, the square was considered the most perfect geometric figure because it consisted of four counterparts to the four primary elements — center, diameter, circumference, and surface — essentially making it a tetrad.

Carl G. Jung (1875–1961), a Swiss psychiatrist and psychoanalyst, discovered from his own dreams and those of his patients, as well as from icons and myths the world over, that fourfold designs such as crosses and squares — especially those linked to the figures he called mandalas — symbolized the search for a center, outwardly in the cosmos and inwardly in the psyche.

Ancient people used to swear by Pythagoras on account of the tetrad, because they were astounded at his discovery of it. Empedocles (490–430 BCE), a Greek pre-Socratic philosopher, once referred to Pythagoras as he "who handed down to our generation the tetraktys, the fount which holds the roots of ever-flowing Nature."[17]

The teachings of François Robichon de la Guérinière (1688–1751), the father of French equitation, continue to form the basis of classical dressage practice. La Guérinière discusses the value of schooling on the square in *École de Cavalerie*. In La Guérinière's own words:

> *The manège, which is considered to be a place where horses are exercised, must be a long square [that is, a large square], and the division of the square into several other larger and smaller forms is what is called the wide "doubler" and the narrow "doubler."*
>
> *Practice on the square made the horse attentive to the aids of the hand and legs, as the rider employed the technique of turning the horse's shoulders at the end of the line of the square without the croup coming out of line. For this, it is necessary, while turning at the end of each line of the square to form a quarter of a circle with the shoulders and to keep the haunches in the same place. In this action, the inside hind leg must remain in one place and the other three legs (the two front and the outside hind leg) must turn in a circular manner around the inside hind, which serves as a pivot. When the shoulders have reached the line of the haunches, one continues to pass straight between the heels to the other corner of the square. This lesson is repeated at the end of each line, except in the corners where the angles of the square are formed by the meeting of the two walls. The haunches must therefore follow*

*in the path of the shoulders; in other words, through
the angles of the corner and at the same time that
the shoulders are turned onto the other line.*[18]

The essence of longitudinal and lateral balance is
contained in the simple exercise of schooling on the
square. Likewise, the rider's fundamental tools of collection are implicit in this technique. The horse's shoulders are freed to become mobile, because the task of
weight-bearing is assigned to the inside hind leg. La
Guérinière didn't need drawreins, chambons, or other
gadgets or shortcuts that allow the rider to sidestep
parts of the training process and get artificial results
from the horse. He had the tetrad.

CHAPTER 2

TRANSCENDENTAL UNION

Contact, Relaxation, Rhythm

*Any path is only a path, and there is no affront, to
oneself or to others, in dropping it if that is what your heart
tells you. . . . Look at every path closely and deliberately. Try it
as many times as you think necessary. Then ask yourself, and
yourself alone, one question. . . . Does this path have a heart?
If it does, the path is good; if it doesn't, it is of no use.*

— **CARLOS CASTANEDA,**
The Teachings of Don Juan

Western social norms, so strongly influenced by the
Puritan ethic, have traditionally offered a distorted
view of sensuality and body communication. Nudity is
regarded with suspicion, touching is associated with
lust, and sharing sensual experience is considered in-
appropriate. In general, appreciation for the body has
been considered pornographic. I recently entered some
of my artwork in a gallery show. In an attempt to decide

which pieces might find favor with the jury, I called the show organizer and asked some questions. I told her that I had a couple of "risky" new works that I would like to enter but was uncertain how the jury would receive them. She asked me what I meant by "risky," and I told her they were abstracts with extremely bold colors and lines. "Oh," she replied, "as long as they're not nudes, I don't think there will be any problems."

Other cultural traditions hold a more integrated view of the human condition: mind, body, and spirit are cohesive and interdependent upon one another for holistic personal growth. The Tantric yogi, for example, considers intimate physical contact to be a means for awakening kundalini, the dazzling life-energy that lies coiled within each of us. According to this view, kundalini, the primal sensual energy that created the cosmos, arouses and uplifts us. The driving force of evolution, it generates love. The raising of kundalini is the mission of the Tantric yogi. The experience, sought for a long time, may come unexpectedly and be overwhelming. Those who have known it say that it dissolves duality, the sense of self and other, and is a complete and limitless union with the divine.[1] The mission of the Tantric yogi and that of the equestrian *ecuyer* are closely aligned.

As I have already discussed, the dressage rider must necessarily let go of self to merge with the horse. The boundaries between horse and rider must dissolve if the two are to experience oneness. While contact (*anlehnung*), relaxation (*losgelassenheit*), and rhythm (*takt*) are all cornerstones of this unity, it is contact that ultimately assures it. Contact is probably one of the least understood principles of dressage. Uniformly, riders think it means how they hold the reins. In the most reduced sense, it does, but more inclusively it refers to every aspect of exchange that takes place between the horse and rider. It implies a mutual relationship based on reciprocity. It ends up being most observable in the rider's hands, but the hands are only a manifestation of the entire position. If the rider's hand position, and consequently contact, is poor, it's because his or her fundamental position is not sufficiently developed. The rider's errors of position are inhibiting the reciprocity between rider and horse, and, in the expanded sense, contact is not established. The best riders have learned that *less is better*. The less they move around, the less they interfere, the less they rely on the technical aids — the less they give credence to duality between horse and self — the better their mounts can perform.

I recently taught a rider how to improve her

collection in canter with her upper-level dressage horse. I repeatedly instructed her to sit still and stop moving around so much. After several such admonitions, Barb finally looked down from her mare and said, "Oh, you mean that *I* have to stop cantering, so that *she* can!?" Exactly!

I studied for years with a wise old studio artist who spent hours complaining to the class that all our work suffered from too much conformity to the rules. He used to say, "Throw the rules out, forget perspective, forget composition...just draw!" When we did, we began to produce. Our fingers and wrists became supple, and we made lines that were soft and feather light. Shade fell where it naturally should, and forms were nicely rounded and symmetrical.

The same advice would be true for most riders: Just throw out the rules and ride! Forget "heels down, heads up" — just ride from a primal place. Let the canter become a waltz, and the trot a suspended lilt. Too many dressage aspirants crippled by analysis paralysis never allow their life energy to uncoil. They analyze every move, every function, every mistake, going over and over it in their minds, dissecting and evaluating it. Everything becomes quantitative, segregated, and isolated. This is not contact, because it emphasizes duality, thereby admitting no authentic reciprocity between horse and rider.

One evening after a discouraging afternoon with a student, I called a colleague for support. I wore my frustration on my sleeve as I asked her, "Why? Why is it so difficult for some people to learn dressage?" She had obviously wrestled with the same question, as her answer was immediate. "Because," she said, "they are too concerned about what their own bodies are doing, and they have forgotten to feel the horse." I hung up and drew a deep breath, knowing what I had to do. I had to help students weed their human gardens of egocentricity, selfishness, and greed. They had to learn that they do not own their dressage. It belongs as much to the horse as it does to them.

Our life force must be unfettered so that we can become free to participate in primal energy. We need to center in our wildness so that the horse can actualize its tameness. "The marks of wildness," say Robert Bly, James Hillman, and Michael Meade, "are love of nature, especially its silence; a voice free to say spontaneous things; an exuberance, a love of the 'edge.'"[2] The wild rider is not like a psychotic, but, in the words of William Butler Yeats, merely "mad as the mist and snow." The wildness of nature is highly sophisticated.

Jung remarked, "It is difficult to say to anybody, you should...become acquainted with your animal, because people think it is a sort of lunatic asylum, they think the animal is jumping over walls and raising hell all over town. Yet the animal...is pious, it follows the path with great regularity.... Only man is extravagant."[3] The civilized eye of humankind has become dulled, unable to comprehend the natural wildness of the planet.

William Blake has said, "The roaring of lions, the howling of wolves, the raging of the stormy sea, and the destructive sword, are portions of eternity, too great for the eye of man."[4] To this list, I would add the thunder of horses' hooves, their flared nostrils when excited, and their heaving flanks at gallop. The practice of the wild is a secret that not all understand. Sometimes blues musicians, abstract artists, and lovers understand it. To cross the abyss from technical equitation to equestrian *art* requires this understanding.

The self must symbolically die. Things that were once done in the world of phenomena must be reenacted in the world of noumena (the world of objects of human inquiry, understanding, or cognition). There is no gnosis (direct experience of the supernatural or divine) without pain. One must come to know dressage not just with the mind but also with the flesh. Intimate, uninhibited contact between horse and rider is a prerequisite. The rider must become comfortable expressing unconditional love for his or her horse, must surrender the very core of his or her own private being, the sense of self. There is no anguish like that of relinquishing one's individuality, one's sense of control: it is beyond words. But for dressage to take its rightful place as an *art de vivre*, the boundaries of personality must dissolve. "To the extent that there is attachment to 'I', 'me', or 'mine', there is no attachment to, and therefore no unitive knowledge of, the divine Ground," says Aldous Huxley.[5]

Dressage practice demands purity of mind. Dressage riders cannot let the hope of attaining certain levels, scores, and awards govern them. Whenever I hear a student lamenting "how far behind" another student she or he is, I know that ego has not yet been properly subjugated. Statements like "If I had her horse I would be doing better" and "He has more natural talent than I do" reveal a covetous, greedy spirit. The mind must be cleansed so that, as the late Henri van Schaik, a Dutch equestrian who competed in the 1936 Summer Olympics, was fond of reminding his students, we can practice "art only for the sake of art." Then, and only then, can dressage become an avenue to reflection, exploration, awareness, and self-knowledge. This is the climate in which relaxation (*losgelassenheit*) can grow.

Breath control and posture are central to relaxation. In Indian philosophy, the term for breath control is *pranayama*, and for posture, *asana*. Both breathing technique and position are as critical to dressage as they are to yoga. How many times has a clinician instructed you to "breathe" and "sit tall"? To become accomplished in either takes considerable practice and presupposes a thorough commitment to spirituality. For as the body progressively relaxes and "lets go," the mind follows by suspending cognition. In this yielded state, the practitioner is extremely inclined toward spiritual insight and becomes aware that dressage offers the experience of attaining transcendental union with a partner. Most other yogic disciplines are yogas-of-one, but dressage is a yoga-of-two.

The union between horse and rider is a sacred sacrifice that teaches each to treat the other with the utmost respect and reverence. The rider discards cruel training tools and brings compassion to the work. The horse gives up her vices, such as bucking, rearing, and bolting, and gains confidence in, and respect for, the process. In *The Ethics and Passions of Dressage,* Charles de Kunffy points out that equestrian sculpture often depicts men in the nude, either seated on horses in antiquity or, in our century, walking alongside their equestrian partners.

> *The horse bares all about his rider. Leaving noth-*
> *ing to the imagination, the rider appears in the*
> *spiritual nudity of utter frankness, stripped of his*
> *pretentious draping. The reciprocity of power and*
> *energy ennobles both creatures beyond the char-*
> *acter they project by themselves. The configuration*
> *of these vastly different creatures as a pair far sur-*
> *passes the potential of their composite parts. They*
> *are more beautiful together than they could ever*
> *be separately.*[6]

The Kubjika Tantra enjoins an adept to worship his lover as a goddess. To the rider, his or her horse becomes sacred and is the object of his or her adoration. We listen to the heartbeat of Pegasus in every stride that we share with our mount. Horse and rider absorb one another's *prana,* or life energy, into their fusing senses. If we can lose ourselves in dressage, become no longer conscious of where our body ends and our horse's body begins, so that the dance itself becomes the only reality, then we may — even if only for an instant — experience magical oneness.

When we are in deep harmony with our horse, rhythm flows naturally. Pythagoras declared, upon the authority of Empedocles, that every individual who is to achieve greatness must be capable of expressing rhythm in some manner. Rhythm (*takt*) in dressage is the metronome-like sound of the horse's footfalls. Rhythm does not exist in a vacuum but is indicative of balance. If the horse suddenly loses its balance and falls on the forehand (the front legs and shoulders), he rushes. Similarly, if balance is compromised by inarticulate rider aids, the horse bears down on the forehand and loses free forward momentum. Rhythm and balance flow from the same well.

Rider position is the key to balance. Pythagoras maintained that anything that departs from its center departs from balance. Teachers such as Sally Swift and Mary Wanless have been instrumental in making riders aware of their centers. Sally Swift writes in *Centered Riding* that, "if you watch someone riding and s/he looks off balance, jerky, or stiff, it is almost always because the center is wrong. The rider is usually behind his/her own balance and behind the motion of the horse. If s/he can get the center correct, the rest will fall into place." Swift goes on to say,

> *To find your center, simply point a finger at your belly to a spot between your navel and your pubic arch, the front of your pelvis. Deep behind that point, against the front of your spine, lies your center of balance, your center of energy, and your center of control. From the bottom of your diaphragm*

and rib cage, large muscles stretch to the lower spine. Other muscles connect from there into the pelvis and down to the thighs. These are some of the deepest and strongest muscles in your body. If you were to cut yourself in half at your center, you would find that, because the lower, or lumbar, vertebrae are very thick, the front of your spine is actually in the center of the circle of your body, not at the back, as you might have thought. Down here, deep and close to the lumbar spine, you also have the largest bundle of muscle-controlling nerves in your body. At the site of this large nerve center and the heavy, controlling muscles, is your center.[7]

Pythagorean theory, based upon mathematical principles, maintained that the stability of a body was destroyed as soon as the vertical line passing through its center of gravity fell outside its base. Pythagorean theory is a perfect description of the classical dressage position! It is also the position of *hamni*, for example, in aikido. When standing in *hamni*, the martial artist is in perfect balance, centered and able to blend efficiently with his or her partner. Likewise, when seated in the classical position, the dressage rider is in perfect balance and absorbs any fractious movement by the horse. This soft, supple position is very secure. The rider, by giving up dominance, gains stability. It is worth noting that both dressage and the martial arts have roots in war and other violent circumstances. In those settings, improper technique could result in death. Consequently, the survival instinct, the desire to maintain immanence with nature, wove the ways of enlightenment into the technique.

My friend Ben is a lifetime student of aikido. He told me he realized just how much was ingrained in the technique when he visited an army base in Japan with an aikido teacher who couldn't speak English. Although the language barrier prevented the master from teaching the underlying philosophy, the students — all American soldiers — were starting to come to all sorts of realizations about centering and blending. Ben excitedly told me that "they were getting it from the technique! No one could explain it to them, but they were getting it anyway — just from training!" On that visit Ben discovered that the basics of centered practice, which result in changed consciousness, went beyond the confines of linguistics: they were implicit in the art. And so it is with dressage. Like the Samurai of ancient Japan, the most eloquent contemporary dressage artists have acquired a complete disdain for force. Says Paul Belasik, "It is as if out of the roots of violence, subjugation and war, these few people seek harmony with nature. They try to create something ephemeral. It is art they can never finish."[8]

Art consists of communication of spirit through form. It's the union of external reality with inner knowledge. From this standpoint, in equestrian art there is no secret so close as that between a dressage artist and his or her horse. An awareness of external reality derives from the study of nature in its totality — from cosmic to microcosmic — and inner knowledge results from reflection. The two are inseparable. Dressage is an avenue in the search for truth and purity, illuminated by the old maxim "Where art ends, violence begins . . . and violence begins where knowledge ends." Horse and rider travel as partners, the rider ever cognizant that, wherever humanity has left its footprint in the long ascent from barbarism to civilization, there is the hoofprint of the horse beside it.

CHAPTER 3

RESPONSIBLE POWER
Impulsion, Straightness, Collection

The age of the utilitarian horse is over. But the horse as an object of art, as a subject of concern, as a monument to character development is now more important than ever. That which is irreplaceable and not interchangeable deserves cherishing.

— CHARLES DE KUNFFY,
The Ethics and Passions of Dressage

When impulsion, straightness, and collection are stirred into the dressage recipe, the result is like a controlled explosion. The dance becomes a hurricane of fresh air, a blend of power and responsibility. After horse and rider have achieved a satisfactory degree of mastery over rhythm, relaxation, and contact, the work that leads to impulsion (*schwung*), straightness (*geraderichten*), and collection (*versammlung*) may begin.

Impulsion is the pushing power of the horse and is created as the horse temporarily stores energy generated by the forward reach of his hind legs. Straightness is an important partner to impulsion, because straightness causes the horse to channel his impulsion directly to his center of balance, giving the rider, who receives the impulsion, or energy, into his or her hands via the reins, a connection to the horse's hindquarters. A horse is considered straight when his hind legs follow the path of his front legs, on both straight and bent lines, and his body is parallel to the line of travel.

Collection is the goal of dressage training. During collection, the horse is asked to take more of her weight onto her hindquarters. The joints of the hind legs demonstrate flexibility, allowing the horse to lower her hindquarters, bring her hind legs further under her body, and lighten her forehand. In essence, collection assumes the horse's ability to move her center of gravity back. If the foundation has been properly built through work with contact, relaxation, rhythm, this new, more advanced work should follow smoothly. If, however, as is often the case, the earlier, utilitarian functions have been shortchanged, serious problems will surface as the rider attempts to develop impulsion, straightness, and collection. Rather than leading to a harmonious controlled explosion, the work will demonstrate either all *control* or all *explosion*. Neither of these individual polarities constitutes dressage.

Impulsion is probably one of the least understood concepts in dressage riding. I have seen riders careening around the edge of the arena at breakneck speeds who claim they are working on impulsion. Nothing, in fact, could be further from the truth. Speed is the enemy of impulsion. Impulsion, in its purest sense, refers to the time the horse spends in the air: it is the degree of suspension that has been developed in the gaits. The horse doesn't just go forward, in the sense of covering ground, but also moves upward. The canter strides become well-defined little jumps, and the trot strides begin to float. In order to facilitate impulsion, the rider must maintain a position correct in both form and function. I have already suggested that dressage is a yoga-of-two. Let's explore some concepts and terminology from the practice of yoga and see how they apply to dressage.

Essential to yogic technique is an *asana*, or posture, that is stable and agreeable. Asana cannot be learned simply from description, but requires the guidance of a perceptive mentor. Mircea Eliade, for example, says,

"The important thing is that asana gives the body a stable rigidity, at the same time reducing physical effort to a minimum."[1] In asana, one does not focus on the irritating feeling of fatigue and of enervation in certain parts of the body, but totally devotes the attention to the fluidity of consciousness. At first, an asana may be uncomfortable and even unbearable. However, after some practice the effort of maintaining the body in the same position becomes minimal. And this perfectly describes the dressage position too.

The classical position, of course, puts the rider in a specific *place*, but it must also give him or her a specific *way*. The dressage seat is concerned not only with *where* a rider sits but also with *how*. I can't begin to recall the number of riders I've worked with who have ridden bolt upright into a lesson. Someone had drilled into them that they must mentally drop a plumb line down through their ears, shoulders, hips, and heels. Some of these riders endured the agony of muscle spasms, contorted vertebrae, and/or damaged ligaments, having achieved the correct physical *form* at the expense of correct physical *function*. They had been forced into an external representation of the position without being taught the underlying qualities of the posture. In short, they had not attained a stable and agreeable seat.

To attain such a seat, effort must disappear and the posture must become natural so that increased sensitivity can occur. The Yoga Sutras of Patañjali say, "Posture becomes perfect when the effort to attain it disappears, so that there are no more movements in the body. In the same way, its perfection is achieved when the mind is transformed into infinity."[2] This mental state requires a complete suspension of attention to the presence of one's own body. The yogic texts give us a perfect description of the classical dressage position!

The Sutras teach that correct asana is a sign of transcending the human condition. It is the first concrete step that the yogi takes for the purpose of abolishing the modalities of human existence. So it is with the dressage rider. I had a student, Sue, who found that the classical position was a constant struggle. Although she mentally gave herself permission to let go, she couldn't get her body to follow. Physical rigidity made it impossible for her to move different parts of her body independently. Her problem was compounded by anxieties developed while under the tutelage of a negative and critical instructor. One day during Sue's lesson, I surreptitiously played some New Age music that had been digitally engineered to enhance inner harmony.

Within a few minutes of riding while listening to these tones, Sue resembled Sally Swift's spruce tree.[3] Her roots had grown down from her center as her trunk had grown up. The celestial sounds of the music had inspired Sue to transcend her human condition. As she softened into a functionally correct position, her horse began to "swing through his back" — meaning his stride was even, his back muscles were soft, and he presented no resistance — with every step, and the gateway to impulsion swung open for both horse and rider.

When the rider is a sack of potatoes astride the horse, impulsion is not possible. Our asana, the classical seat, must find soft and supple expression. Once the posture has become established, the rider is ready to practice proper breathing, another tool for improving the quality of the dressage position. Systematic breathing, or *pranayama*, prepares the mind for concentration by making it steady. The Sutras teach that, when the breath moves, the mind also moves. Likewise, when the breath ceases to move, the mind becomes motionless. And yogic tradition teaches that when the breath does not move, the body becomes as *stiff as a stump*. The real significance of pranayama is that it controls the nerve centers that cause the respiratory muscles to alternately relax and contract. The breath itself has very little to do with it, though the art of breathing is a primary means of bringing our nervous impulses under control.

Pranayama, then, really signifies the control of energy, of the impulses of the automatic nervous system and the numerous activities of the body caused by them.[4] The dressage rider able to control his or her nervous impulses becomes softer, making it easier for the horse to carry him or her. Concurrently, the rider's mind opens to the artistic and/or spiritual experience. From this place, the rider is capable of practicing both objective and subjective concentration.

The word "concentration" refers to the center. In thought, "concentrating" is the act of bringing the mind to a single point. Objectively, the mind is aimed at concentrating on a point outside the body, subjectively, on a point within the body. The rider must practice both forms of concentration in order to maintain balanced, harmonious growth.[5] I have found that most riders are well schooled in objective concentration — too much so, in fact. They are comfortable working with facts, figures, and empirical observation, but the concept of subjective concentration is more foreign.

Subjective concentration allows us to go deep within ourselves. It is quietly introspective and intuitive.

It simply finds what is and makes no judgments. Subjective concentration might more accurately be called contemplation. A Plotinian flavor is found in the realization that the whole hierarchy of spiritual reality exists within the individual human soul, and that it can be accessed through contemplation, through the exploration of the self in its complexity.[6] We attain a better understanding of the intricate tapestry of dressage when we forgo the application of physical aids — the cues that riders give horses — which keep us cognitive, and we become contemplative instead. When riders obsess over correctly applying physical aids to the exclusion of any other consideration (such as harmony, balance, and so on), they focus on the physical, asking themselves questions like: "Did I give my leg aid at the right moment?" "Was my rein aid too strong?" When this happens, they forget the big picture.

Alexander of Aphrodisias, head of the Peripatetic Lyceum in Athens at the start of the third century CE, distinguished between two kinds of intelligible form — one immanent in matter, and one transcendent — and two intellects, one passive and one active. Whereas immanent forms are known when the mind interacts with sensory data, transcendent forms are known when the mind identifies with the universal intelligence. The latter way-of-knowing requires no empirical, or objective, data. It is a primal knowledge base that is evident and operative in, for example, children and animals. As riders begin to actualize subjective concentration, or contemplation, this type of communication happens with greater frequency between them and their horses.

This is the realm in which, as Dominique Barbier and Mary Daniels point out, visualization takes place: "People ride the way they are, mentally, emotionally, spiritually. That is why horses perform differently for different riders."[7] We are what we think. According to Robert Masters, "Our brains respond to images quite literally. Imagined events have a physical effect. If you image hard physical exertion, your heart will begin to race. Experiments have shown that our inner vision is subject to the same optical illusions as our outer." When a person is fully relaxed, "the brain is unable to distinguish between images and objective reality."[8]

I used to know an old Colombian man who could ride any horse well, no matter how difficult. Under Carlos, spooky horses became brave, nervous ones grew calm, and lazy horses perked up with interest. Whenever someone asked Carlos what the secret to his success was, he would just grin and say that he loved horses and he loved riding. It never took a horse long to figure this out. When Carlos mounted up, his mind wasn't cluttered with objective *what ifs*. He swung into the saddle with the image of a pleasant ride on a happy horse — and that is what he always got. One of my teachers, the late Chuck Grant, loved to remind his students that dressage horses were very simple to understand. He would say matter-of-factly, "They go the way they're ridden!"[9]

Elegant dressage riders practice subjective concentration. They know how to use positive imagery. They've learned a lot about themselves because they've spent time in their own centers. They've found that still, quiet place within, where they can listen to the inaudible and see the invisible. When we ride with subjective concentration, we radiate tranquility and confidence to the horse. The horse mirrors our peacefulness and moves more freely forward and upward. Impulsion increases when we stop objectively concentrating on making it happen and simply allow it to happen. When our concentration is too objective, impulsion is stifled — our analysis paralysis becomes so devastating that it could subtract forward motion in a runaway horse.

Correctly developed impulsion is evident when the horse's withers elevate. All too often in contemporary dressage, riders inadvertently crush down their horses' withers. These unfortunate horses aren't allowed to "work softly through their toplines" — that is, their backs aren't gently rounded, without tension, as they should be — but are instead jammed into the bit by a combination of forceful driving aids and simultaneous, strong rein contact. More often than not, such a horse is presented in a tightly fitted cavesson (a leather strap fitted over the top of the bit and around the nose) and a flash noseband (a leather strap fitted under the bit and around the horse's nose). Whereas the baroque dressage style was guilty of crushing and overly bending the rear end of the horse, the contemporary dressage style compresses the front end of the horse. Prevented from lifting their withers and wrapping themselves around the bit, these poor animals are literally contracted between hand and heel. Although they may give the impression of being in the correct "outline" — that is, in a relaxed, balanced position that allows for efficient movement — they are not. Their backs are inverted and tense, so impulsion is impossible.

Have you ever watched a mare in the field groom her foal's withers? As the mare works her youngster's withers with her muzzle and teeth, the foal elevates his withers, pushing them up for grooming. He also loosens his lower jaw and begins to make chewing gestures, salivating and softly moving his lips. He looks as if he's talking and smiling, making pleasant facial movements. This same comfort should be evident in the horse being ridden: the horse should elevate her withers and relax her lower jaw, chewing and softly gesticulating with her lips and tongue. The two actions — being ridden and gesticulating — go hand in hand. Jean-Claude Racinet, a popular and successful teacher and trainer, has diligently pointed out the importance of the sternohyoid muscle in equine locomotion, which links the tongue to the sternum. Racinet cites the research of Nancy Nicholson, a biologist at Miami University in Oxford, Ohio, saying, "The relaxed jaw allows the geniohyoid muscle at the base of the tongue which is embedded in the front projection of the hyoid apparatus (which, in turn, is connected at its lower back end to the sternum) to respond to the most refined dialogue between bit and tongue."[10]

In artistic equitation, therefore, soft articulations of the jaw are evidence of liberated withers, through which the energy of impulsion may move without restriction. Once the horse is pushing powerfully forward and upward, the rider may address straightness to ensure that the impulsion will not be interrupted. One way to think about this is to visualize the horse as a conduit through which the impulsive energy flows. If the conduit becomes twisted or crooked at any point, this impedes the flow of energy. When this happens, we say the horse is not permeable. Permeability, the quality of relaxation that allows the horse's muscles to give in to the motion, so that the rider's aids go freely "through" the horse, is fundamental to proper dressage practice and, when lost, must be restored.

The method for restoring permeability is called straightening, which entails the equilateral employment of the horse's skeletal and muscular systems. Its goal is to facilitate the horse's acceptance of an even workload throughout its body. The work of straightening helps the horse employ a full range of motion as it discovers the most efficient use of its muscles and joints. The rider straightens the horse through methodical work with lateral, or sideways, movements: shoulder-in, haunches-in, half-pass. These movements invite the horse to use his body in an equilateral, balanced way, by progressively putting his weight on his haunches instead of on the forehand, where horses naturally carry more of their weight. The horse shifts his weight toward the rear quarters, thereby liberating his shoulders. The liberation of the shoulders and forehand are an essential prerequisite for collection.

However, the work of liberation is not confined to biomechanics.

The lateral movements are, in fact, tools that liberate the rider from his or her egoistic I-ness. Well executed, the lateral movements appear effortless, like a finely choreographed dance. Under a master artist, it appears as if the horse has chosen to undertake these movements silently and peacefully with no urging from the rider. The creative power of art is evidenced in the luminous silence and the expression of spontaneity. In this state, the individual will is liberated to identify with the creative will. Through this identification, the spirit discards its I-ness by engaging with divine light and power. By means of the lateral movements, dressage recovers the life impulse in spirituality. The vital, aesthetic impulses acquire true meaning when they become spiritual expression.

After straightness is accomplished, the rider may ask the horse to collect, which is the ultimate goal of dressage. From a strictly biomechanical standpoint, collection is the progressive loading of the horse's hindquarters. The horse can set on her hindquarters only the amount of weight that her hindquarters can carry (relative to the degree of strength), according to her fitness and strength. Whereas straightness facilitates liberation, collection is where all the inherent aesthetic qualities of the dressage experience meet. Dressage then becomes contemplation (*theoria*), or prayer. "Contemplation is that condition of alert passivity," says Huxley, "in which the soul lays itself open to the divine Ground within and without, the immanent and transcendent Godhead."[11] This is a state of union with all being.

The highest contemplation is, of course, the most passive, for the less there is of self, the more there is of the All. As Evelyn Underhill puts it, "That dreadful consciousness of a narrow and limiting I-hood which dogs our search for freedom and full life, is done away with. For a moment, at least, the independent spiritual life is achieved."[12] This experience is given rather than attained: it is an experience of the beautiful. While engaged in it, the rider is aware of his or her own littleness, unworthiness, and ignorance in comparison with the ineffable greatness of the beautiful. This is a state of perfect love, from which joy, confidence, affection, and awe naturally flow. In this state of nondual consciousness, the rider is freed from any desires of conquest.

Aesthetics is a path for discovering the integration of

these spiritual forces, one that allows them to establish creative harmony so that one's consciousness can expand. "Art is creative and also relative. It gives a definite spiritual attitude which awakens the dormant forces dominant in us, by making them useful for realization of the divine wisdom,"[13] says Pranab Bandyopadhyay. The value of the dressage experience lies in acquainting the rider with the spiritual architecture of the universe, the immanent radiant forces and divine transcendence in the heart of existence. Dressage, as an art, has the potential to facilitate the transformation of deep insight into spirituality.

Bandyopadhyay's sentiments about the tantras are equally applicable to dressage:

> *An exquisite artistic display is seen when the spirit releases the dormant creative forces and activates them in all the strata of our being: mental, vital and sub-vital, and ultimately infuses them with higher inspiration and starts a new orientation of our being. This fine art makes the forces active in order that divinity may counteract upon the earth and gradually instill its influence into it. This great spiritual venture is the finest expression of the creative act of spirit. Life emerges in its dignity and*

beauty. Man is made a supreme specimen of the divine art in creation.[14]

The person who is a "supreme specimen of the divine art in creation" has necessarily experienced transformation.

THE HYMN OF LOVE

Balance, Harmony, Freedom

It is rare to see a rider who is truly passionate about the horse and his training, taking a profound interest in dressage with self-abnegation, and making this extraordinarily subtle work one of the dominant motivations in his life.

— **NUNO OLIVEIRA,**
Reflections on Equestrian Art

Our evolution into a higher and broader identity is driven by eros, by the discovery of a greater union. Eros, as the Greek philosopher Plato used the term, is essentially self-transcendence, the very motor of spiritual development. Eros is the power in love that unites things that are different. The object of eros is beauty. Agape is compassion that expresses itself when an individual gives care to one who requires it and who is not as well off as the giver. Eros and agape together complete a vast circle of love not confined to one place or one time, but which has the qualities of infinity and/or eternity implicit within it. At each stage of development, the lower individual — the one not as well off — must be embraced and permeated, so that descent, or movement from the gods to matter, occurs with each stage of ascent, or movement from matter to the gods. Eros, or transcendental wisdom, must be balanced with agape, or unconditional acceptance, at every step along the path.

No part of the dressage journey is about eros, nor is any part of it about agape. It's about their integration. In this journey, we can reach an impasse that seems insurmountable. We can feel alienated from the healing and nurturing energies of archetypal love. Awkward canter pirouettes or clumsy half-passes can throw up roadblocks that stop us cold. But we can turn these moments into experiences of *lux e tenebris* (light out of darkness). The decisions we make determine whether our world will become richer and fuller or shatter under the burden of despair. A theory in quantum physics posits that the entire universe is made of light, that the tiny quanta called photons, or particles of light, compose every palpable, visible aspect of creation. According to this theory, light not only is a means of seeing but also is seeing itself.

Light is accessed through an attitude of love. Very simply, we approach love through the practice of balance, harmony, and freedom. Without these disciplines, our sight is limited and finite. Darkness is not the antithesis of light, but a property of light, its inner density.[1] Seen from this perspective, choices become easier to make.

Balance, harmony, and freedom are interdependent and flow naturally from one to the other. If any one of these qualities is not attended to, the other two will also suffer. I often hear riders complaining that their horses are not in balance. It's probably a very good thing that horses can't talk! Our horse is our mirror, and if it's out of balance, so are we. In dressage, balance does not stop at the physical periphery but interfaces with our mind and our spirit and becomes a springboard for the joy of the soul. The soul is not dedicated to perfection but instead appreciates human limitation and folly.[2] Life is a play of opposites: in the heart of one thing lives its opposite. An embryo growing in a woman's womb is not her, yet is sustained by her body. To love and trust another living being, to engage respectfully in mutual growth, is constantly to be open to another point of view.[3]

I once had a student whose riding style was tantamount to one prolonged argument with her horse. She refused to even consider the horse's point of view.

Placing strenuous demands on her horse, whose fitness and coordination were too poorly developed to allow him to obey her orders, she would become angry at his "resistance" to her requests. Anytime I tried to point out that most horses' refusals were symptoms of physical discomfort, suggesting that she have her veterinarian assess his conditioning and feeding program, she would angrily insist that the horse was simply stubborn. Her claim that "he just didn't want to do it" was an easy way out of having to look at her own personal imbalances. If, instead of hiding behind denial, she had been able to see her horse's point of view, a dialogue could have begun that could have given her an opportunity to work toward personal balance.

The *I Ching*, or *Book of Changes*, teaches us that the elements of life constantly grow toward their fullest possibility, then change into their opposite. The emblem for the interflow of yin and yang is called the Tao, which means the Way, characterized by a circle divided by a curved line from top to bottom and left to right, with one side of the line light and the other side dark. We can see the essential nature of balance when we note the small circle of pure light in the center of the dark side and the small circle of pure dark in the center of the light. Although the two sides are fundamentally opposed, each intimately knows the other because it contains its antithesis: it holds the other in its heart.

In the dance of dressage, as with the Tao, we learn not only that we contain our opposites but also that we *are* our opposites. It becomes the task of the rider to seek out his or her horse and embrace that which — in the horse — differs from the rider, and then find the bond of sameness between them. At the intrapersonal level, this dance takes place between our conscious and unconscious selves. We dance with our shadow whenever we experience inner conflict. However, resolution comes if we dance long enough. When we learn to stop struggling and move into a process of dialogue, something new can happen. Then, and only then, can we come into balance.

Balance is kinetic and can't be found in the same place twice. Yesterday's balance is stale today. The dialogue contains an infinite continuum of opposites. When a common ground is found, synthesis results. However, to define this synthesis as permanent causes the process to stagnate. Instead, let the synthesis become a new thesis, one prepared to dance with its new antithesis until yet another synthesis is found. When we do this, we are Tao dancing, fully aware that the music will never stop.

When we begin to attain personal balance, harmony becomes the next frontier. Ancient Greek thought posited the musical scale as a utopian model of proportion and harmony bridging the gap between the high notes and the low notes. It encapsulated the most fundamental pattern of harmonic symmetry and demonstrated that the phenomena of nature were tied to one another through the principle of reciprocity.[4]

In dressage, though we spend a lot of time talking about harmony, we don't actually find it demonstrated very often. What we see instead is a type of pathology centered on issues of power. Slowly, quietly, and often insidiously, the rider becomes dominant while the horse habitually submits to his or her authority. In some cases, power is tossed back and forth between horse and rider, but the transaction is so uneven that the rider always emerges as dominant. In some cases the pathology of such a relationship is manifested dramatically.

For example, I once gave a lesson to a woman who suddenly and without any apparent provocation unleashed a torrent of anger on her horse. While shouting obscenities, she whipped him abusively. After I urgently implored her to stop, she finally consented and then turned her rage on me. When she finally regained enough composure that I was able to ask her what was going on, I learned that she was furious with her husband and had brought this anger into her riding as displaced aggression. She had systematically conditioned her horse to serve as a whipping boy when her emotional instability overcame her. In asserting dictatorial dominance over the horse, she rendered him powerless. Harmony cannot be expressed or experienced in this kind of relationship.

In dressage, great value is placed on the horse's submission. Submission, however, radically differs from broken-willed subservience. The submissive horse is a "willing slave" who performs her job happily because she knows that the rider will, in turn, reciprocate in attending, as a "willing slave," to the horse's day-to-day custodial needs. We build harmony as a result of relinquishing control. But this yielding presents its own set of problems. My years of teaching dressage have shown me that most people's initial attraction to the precision and order of the art arises from a control agenda. I once heard a colleague challenge a new dressage student by saying, "If you try to tell me that you're not a control freak, I'm going to call you a liar!" She, too, had been teaching dressage long enough to know that the new rider's control agenda was the first dragon the rider needed to slay.

Charles de Kunffy tells us that the harmonious

submission of a horse to the rider's will begins with "the replacement of inborn instinct-dictated reactions in the animal with rider-inspired reactions."[5] As the horse begins to trust her rider, submission naturally follows. The rider can never demand or force this trust but must earn it. It will develop with the rider's kindness, patience, understanding, reasonableness, and above all, consistency. In this fertile soil, harmony will sink its roots. The wise rider knows that the flower that blooms the longest is never one that was forced open.

When we interact harmoniously with our horses, our instructors, and our riding peers, we begin to experience what the philosopher Martin Buber called I-Thou relationships.[6] These relationships connect harmony with freedom. The dressage student's first introduction to an I-Thou relationship is at the hand of his or her teacher. The masterful teacher knows that a reciprocal I-Thou relationship between teacher and student involves a state of grace. Always ready to give and receive, understanding the tenuousness of the moment, the teacher-of-the-art must constantly work toward helping the student realize his or her potential. An aware teacher accepts the student as the composite person he or she is, both actually and potentially: the student is not merely a sum of qualities, strivings, and inhibitions but is a whole being, and the teacher affirms this wholeness. But this process can occur only if teacher and student meet repeatedly as partners in a polarized situation. As the teacher experiences situations both from his or her own viewpoint and from that of the student, transactions become useful and inspiring. This is the kind of realization that Buber called "inclusion" (*Umfassung*).[7]

When the dressage student has such a gifted teacher, he or she experiences a sense of inclusion and can then replicate this model relationship when working with a horse. Cognizant of the grace in a reciprocal relationship, the perceptive rider allows a shared energy — a result of their partnership — to flow between himself or herself and the horse, staying in the moment, neither dwelling on the past nor anticipating the future. A spoiled halt or poor transition is over — gone — and the rider must let it go. Concurrently, the tempi — performed when a horse changes leads at the canter while in the air between two strides — will not be improved by anticipation. We can only ride in this moment: now. Only through a continual series of "nows" does the rider develop the horse's potential. In this context, the rider accepts the horse as she actually is, rather than as the rider wants her to be. The horse, then, is seen not as a conglomerate of individual qualities but as a whole.

Harmony cannot grow between horse and rider if the horse is constantly being evaluated on isolated performance abilities. When I hear, for example, a rider complaining about a poor extended trot and extolling the collected work, I know that this rider is not working or thinking in terms of the whole. Extension and collection cannot be segregated, either in theory or in practice. These two functions are interdependent. When either is in peril, the other is necessarily affected, and until the rider finds the problem with the whole, things will not improve. In harmonics, C is not fully actualized apart from E or G. Harmony requires allowing individual qualities to integrate. C is free to be C only when it's tuned, for example, to E. If we negate the harmony in any situation, we rob it of its freedom.

A horse who has been robbed of its freedom — the freedom of its presence and brilliance, the freedom of its gaits, the freedom of its full range of motion, and the freedom of its kindness — is tragic. Balance ushers in harmony, and harmony gives birth to freedom, which completes the cycle, bringing us back to love. Freedom and love are synonymous. Each has responsibilities born of ethics, but neither is limited or finite.

Several years ago, I began teaching a woman who was not free: she was held captive by multiple sclerosis. Dressage had always been the most important thing in Kayla's life, and now she faced losing her dream. As her physical condition deteriorated and she lost more and more neuromuscular control, she became despondent. She wrote me a letter saying, "The very foundation of my own identification is cracked and falling beneath me. I am lost and floundering . . . and terribly, terribly afraid. My grief is almost unbearable."

I was teaching Kayla from an I-Thou perspective and had helped her achieve a significant degree of inclusion (*Umfassung*) in her process. I knew where I had to guide her. I stopped addressing the technical aids — the journeyman's tools — and began focusing on, sometimes even subliminally, freedom and love. I helped her initiate a new apprenticeship. Progress was slow but steady. Working with Kayla and her horse was like looking into a crystal ball: I could see exactly what was going on inside her and what dragons she would be slaying next. There were times I had to be completely silent so she could own what was happening. "Loquacity," said Apollonius, a first-century philosopher who espoused Neopythagoreanism, "has many pitfalls, but silence none."

I knew Kayla was standing at the portal of freedom when I read her next letter, about the growth and improvement in her riding. She said, "The love and gratitude I felt for you in that Moment, and the fulfillment of my heart and soul, must have reverberated all the way to you." She had the vision, but needed to assume full ownership of her accomplishments. They were rightfully hers; my job was drawing to a close. And she assumed that ownership a few months later in yet another letter. I had just given her a lesson during which I could feel the energy between Kayla and her horse. It was light, free, powerful energy alive with love. She was riding gracefully, and her horse was dancing with her.

As the lesson unfolded, I grew progressively more passive. Finally, I assumed total silence. Anything I could have said would only have interrupted her ownership of the experience. I knew I had catalyzed her freedom when I read her next letter a few days later. "He [her horse] transcended himself; I transcended myself, and a third entity was born . . . we became One. And, of course, there was Love. It crisscrossed that arena almost palpably. Could you feel it? Love really is the key, isn't it? So, thank you!" Kayla had been set free.

I'd thought this was the end of Kayla's story, but

it wasn't. Later that same year, Kayla wrote the following verses for the horses and horse people who had kept her walking:

Anger and fear set aside now,
I'm ready to do my part;
I can't believe this tide of Love,
That's filling up my heart.
One of you was always there,
Ready to rescue me;
When my life was filled with darkness,
Hopelessness all I could see.

Not only had Kayla been set free, but she was also getting well. She regained the feeling in her legs, got new strength and stamina, and began walking normally. Her physical body was responding to her spiritual transformation. This was a blue ribbon that had nothing to do with a competitive sport. This one would never fade.

CHAPTER 5

THE PATH OF THE SOUL

Forward and Upward

Dive deeply enough into any subject and the questions that shimmer before you are spiritual.

— **JACK HAWLEY,**
Reawakening the Spirit in Work

Dressage provides a means of quintessential spiritual expression, a road map for finding the soul's path. In dressage, we discover that love is the primary catalyst for the soul's ascension. The guiding ideas of forward and upward are primers on the soul's return to the good as we ride toward the highest goal of all: to achieve likeness to, and union with, the One.

A good blueprint for achieving this union is Plotinus's metaphysics. These metaphysics may be considered in two ways: as a progression downward from the One to the world (the divine hypostases), and upward from the world to the One (morality). Plotinus's hypostases, also known as emanations, are marked by four degrees: matter, world soul, nous, and the One. The first divine hypostasis (emanation of the divine) is the prime source and principle of all being whatsoever and is called the One.[1] Plotinus likened it to a stream that is its own source.[2] The One is the principle of all knowledge, and all things are dependent on it. It is above all understanding. The universe proceeds from the One, not by free and willing creation, but by constant emanation. Through these emanations the One participates in all other degrees of reality.

To explain the hypostases, or emanations, Plotinus compared them to the superabundance of a flowing river and to a beam of light. Just as a beam of light grows weaker as it reaches farther from its source, finally vanishing into darkness, so it is with the hypostases, which, after leaving the One, lose their unity and finally vanish into matter.

The first emanation is the nous, which is pure intelligence, or unchanged thoughts. The nous is inferior to the One, since multiplicity starts with nous. The second emanation is the world soul. It proceeds from the nous, as the nous proceeds from the One, and is therefore inferior to the nous. The third and final emanation is matter. Human souls, once in a state of preexistence in the nous, are now imprisoned in a material body. In each individual soul, there are two activities, the rational and informative virtues. The rational tends to the formation of ideas, while the informative tends to the body.

The world soul perpetually revolves about and within the sphere of the nous, from which it emanated, aspiring to the One through the medium of the beautiful.[3] Beauty is a form of intelligence, or nous. Dressage is an outer garment of the beautiful, and as such it lies within the sphere that the individual soul occupies and revolves around. It's what the Ancient Greeks called *kalos k'agathos*, that which is beautiful and correct.

The correctness of dressage is determined by the effects of the work upon the horse's body and mind. If the horse is progressively strengthened and suppled, the work is correct. If, on the other hand, the animal becomes stiffer, losing free range of motion, the training is not following correct principles. A bulging underneck, subluxated spine, and overdeveloped pectoral muscles indicate poor gymnastic technique. Correct dressage technique relaxes the horse, making her quiet and content. The correctly ridden horse has no resistances. She doesn't shy, buck, rear, or bolt, but trots happily and confidently around the school while accepting without resistance the cues the rider supplies. A horse who is nervous, balky, or irritable tells us that the work is not going well. Her dull eyes, flat gait, and chattering teeth are clear signs that we are on the wrong path.

Work that is not functionally correct damages the animal by reducing its potential and, therefore, can never be beautiful. Beauty cannot coexist with tension, stiffness, or exhaustion. There is nothing beautiful in personal greed, ego-centered behavior, or unrealistic goal-setting. Continued participation in the beautiful requires love. In studying dressage, we can begin either at the bottom, with practice and technique; or at the top, with a consideration of metaphysical truths; or even in the middle, at the focal point where mind and matter, action and thought, have their meeting place in human psychology.

I remember one day, after several years of study, when my teacher said, "Riding dressage is not like playing tennis. You can make your body learn the techniques and make your head learn the movements, but the dressage comes from *inside* of you. You really need to develop your *inner* life." This was a turning point for me: I made a quantum leap in my conscious process. I began to understand that people rode according to the way they were, mentally, emotionally, and spiritually, and that this was why horses performed differently for different riders. As we open ourselves up to transformation, our riding improves. One of my riding students recently demonstrated her awareness of this concept when she told me, "You aren't teaching me how to ride; you're teaching me how to live!"

We fail to realize that mastery is not about perfection but about a process, a journey. "The master is the one who stays on the path day after day, year after year," says George Leonard. "The master is the one who is willing to try, and fail, and try again, for as long as he or she lives."[4] Mastery is, and will continue to be, elusive until riders abandon the reductionistic, antisacred, materialistic way of thinking that has dominated Western culture for the last two or three thousand years. The purpose of training a horse is to participate in the beautiful and requires love.

Plotinus defines love as the desire to be united with a beautiful object and, in this way, produce or create beauty. Love is always the result of an affinity, conscious or otherwise, between the soul of the lover and object of his or her passion. Our desire to produce is the outcome of the soul's instinctive craving for immortality, since the essence of immortality is none other than beauty itself.

The best riders I've known are those who have been passionately in love with their horses and their art. There is an emotional nature in us that is free of the ego, and that we can touch when we are in love. The love relationship, says Ken Wilber, is the path of ascent, "which is driven by *eros*, by Love, by the finding of greater and greater union — a higher and wider identity."[5] By means of eros, the partners are taken out of themselves and joined in a larger union with the beautiful. Eros continues to develop from the body to the mind to the soul, until final union is accomplished. Eros "is essentially self-transcendence," says Wilber, "the very motor of ascent or development of evolution: the finding of an ever-higher self-identity with the ever-wider embrace of others."[6]

The aim of eros is to establish an ever greater unity, to bind together. Plotinus reminds us that, at each stage of ascent, the lower being also has to be embraced and integrated. In an integrated process, descent occurs with every stage of ascent. Descent is agape, the higher being reaching down and compassionately embracing the lower, and agape balances eros, or transcendental wisdom, at each and every stage of development. Eros is our passion for our horse and for our art. It is sensuous, heady, and sweet. It is our delight in the intricate movements and the secrets we share with our horse. But eros without agape would be chaos, since agape causes us to feel compassion for our horse and to express it in our art. It makes us feel humble, contrite, and forgiving and causes us to keep no scores and remember no wrongs.

Eros is fueled by the differences between horse and rider. It's excited when we dance with our shadow, and it's aroused by the attraction between opposites. Without the help of agape, eros would have no permanence: it would be too tumultuous to achieve stability. Agape tempers our passion, our zeal, and puts things into a balanced perspective. Agape keeps us patient as an overly eager horse pulls on us, or when a fractious youngster tests the limits. Agape shows us love-in-spite-of, while eros lets us indulge in love-because-of. Our heart sings to our horse, "I love you because of your big, bold trot" and, simultaneously, "I love you in spite of your impatient halt."

Although contemplating and desiring the One are the essential activities of the universal soul, the universal soul's powers are not exhausted by this effort. The generative power that proceeds from the essence of the universal soul is embodied as nature and, as an image of the principal power, is therefore an inferior entity. Everything in nature possesses an individual soul that, like the universal soul of which it is a member, contemplates the intelligible order. However, by virtue of its irrational or strictly natural soul, it is in immediate vital or sympathetic relationship with the rest of the material universe.

The universal soul is also regarded as the principle of nature. It is both one and many. It seeks to reconcile the extremes of integrity and aloofness, of universality and individualization. In the universal intelligence, this reconciliation of opposites, which appears in nature as a perpetual, albeit never accomplished, process, is absolute and eternal. Nature is both unity and multiplicity.

The human mind can be satisfied only by that which simultaneously appeals to and satisfies the heart as well. We choose our horses primarily with our hearts. When we look for a horse, we walk past a dozen perfectly satisfactory candidates until we find one that we see as beautiful. Our inner self knows when we have found beauty. Our soul, which formerly experienced rapture — when we were still united with the One — renounces its attitude of coldly admiring impartiality, awakens invigorated, and expands under the sweet influence of love. Liberated, the soul soars by the aid of reminiscence and adopts a higher principle. Instead of loving a particular person or thing, it loves the One, which is all things and yet no thing. This ecstatic reunion with the good leaves the soul permanently beautified and enlightened and is an act of contemplation of all existence.

The good is the soul's ultimate goal. It is the source or goal of all things, the principle of evolution and involution, and the expulsive energy and the attractive force. It is the ultimate anthropic principle, the circle that closes with itself. In one word, it is love. This is the sole principle of ascension. However, souls that have contemplated the good may return to reveal to others the secret of celestial rapture, which seems to justify the conclusion that love is, or at least should be, also the principle of descension. The individual soul knows no rest until it has completed its circuit and returned to the source it derived from. Duality is overcome as the soul achieves unity with the good. The manège offers us a place to practice integrating the "I" by understanding our responsibilities and freedoms. We integrate the "we" as well by undertaking the relationship between our self and our horse. And we integrate the "it" by becoming aware of the implicit ethics, beauty, and truth in the tradition.

Our entrance into the dressage sanctuary requires us to withdraw into the darkness of our inner space, a darkness that is pregnant with potential. Our horse mirrors our inner space, making us aware of infinite possibility. It can be frustrating for a rider to catch glimpses of this potential and know that it's not being actualized. The harder the rider works, the worse things get. Actualization cannot occur until the rider lets go of his or her control agenda and begins to develop a centaurlike vision-logic — an expanded, integrated consciousness — as the guiding principle. The mythical centaur, half human and half horse, is a symbol of the integration of body and mind, and every time we sit on a horse, we confront the need to integrate our physical and mental selves. The rider must actively value his or her relationship with the horse, acknowledging him as the vehicle for self-discovery. The work becomes a *solve et coagula* (process of separating and rejoining), in which the rider's limited sense of self is dissolved and replaced with an expanded vision of his or her potential. In this sense, dressage is like an alchemical retreat process: the dissolution allows the death of unwanted aspects of the ego and is followed by regeneration.

Alchemy, as a spiritual tradition, was a means for exploring the inner layers that clothe the precious essence of one's innermost soul.[7] It was a path, a way for investigating the substance of one's being. Ancient alchemists used retorts, or crucibles, to heat, calcine, sublime, and distill substances, ever attentive to the transformations that occurred during their experiments. They used events in their experiments as seed images for meditations, forming visual mantras from the chemical changes. The alchemists reflected and mirrored these outward events in their interior world. They saw the processes in their flasks as interactions and links between the spiritual and the material. The spirit rose up, separating from the substance at the bottom of the flask, and descended again to spiritualize the material into an essence or tincture.

As the alchemists reworked these experiments in their souls, they drew further parallels with the greater laboratory of nature. They saw their work as a kind of microcosm of macrocosmic nature. As they began to picture animal symbols for the living alchemical process, they saw living energies and beings in nature as being metaphorically drawn into their retorts. Each stage of the individual's regenerative process was marked by a meeting with a certain animal. Each of the animals represented an archetype for that particular phase of the process. This idea can illuminate dressage if we use it to look at the different horses we have had at various points in our lives. As we look back with uncompromising honesty, we can see that, during each developmental phase, we chose horses that mirrored what was going on in our inner selves.

As the alchemists worked with their retorts, we work with our horses. As they watched for transformations in their alchemical experiments, we should watch for them in our dressage. We should use our observations of these changes to form positive visualizations, just as the alchemists used them as seed images for meditations. As we refine our visualization technique, we reflect these external transformations in our inner lives. For example, I remember a young rider who found that executing a shoulder-in created an imbalance, an unequal lateral weight distribution. Once aware of the problem, she began to conform to a proper projected mental image. Soon she was, once again, perfectly seated and in harmony with her horse and its movements. Further, a sudden insight let her realize that she was not only physically rebalanced and relaxed but that several inner tensions had simultaneously been resolved. In this way, dressage provided an interactive link between the spiritual and material aspects of her process.

At each stage in our journey, we choose — generally subconsciously — horses that reflect the issues that block us from free forward movement. It's interesting to consider our horses in terms of alchemical animal symbolism. The animal metaphors of the European alchemists developed into a universal language, as key alchemical manuscripts circulated widely. It was, in fact, the coherence and universality of this set of alchemical symbols that led Carl Jung to the concept of the collective unconscious.

The phase that alchemists called blackening usually marked the beginning of alchemical work and was symbolized by the black crow or dragon. The alchemists' first task was to make calcine, a substance that would become the "philosopher's stone," and they called this the phase of "profound darkness." Alchemists saw this phase — the meeting with the black crow — as a good omen, because it marked the beginning of the journey. Anyone who has worked in dressage at all has met the black crow. Our black crow comes in the form of a trained schoolmaster who makes us painfully aware of what we do not know.

The blackening is followed by the whitening phase, represented by the white swan or eagle. The white swan is at home on the surface of the water, yet feeds on the dark, muddy bottom of the stream or lake. The swan's whiteness contrasts with the mud, making it a fine symbol of how spiritual purity can be gained from uncompromising primal material. In the whitening phase, we sense the end of the work. It represents a polar swing out of the blackening, and in this phrase the seeds of one's future work are planted. It is a stage of catharsis after an intense experience of being consumed in the crucible, when we glimpse the appearance, however fragmentary, of a new possibility — a flickering light that draws us toward this new possibility's promise of change, of transformation. We are astride the white swan when we begin to see the difference between passion and obsession, mindfulness and control, liberty and anarchy. This is the horse who teaches us that nothing is gained until everything is given up. We never forget the horse who was our white swan.

During the whitening stage, alchemists would often encounter what they called the peacock's tail, a sudden rush of colors, an iridescence on the surface of the material in the flask that made some think they had achieved their goal. But this fleeting show of color changes only pointed to the fact that one was on the right path. At the beginning of the alchemical process, polarities would emerge as disintegrated, separate elements, but as the process continued they would become integrated. The alchemical process would reabsorb and reunite the initially disintegrated polarities of "this" and "that" which had emerged in the first phase of the process. Many riders arrive at just such a midway point and falsely assume they have reached the end of their work. The inner vision of the peacock's tail, beautiful though it may be, is merely a digestion of the polarities of the black and white stages, and these polarities must be commingled even further if we are to have any permanent transformation within the soul. We encounter the peacock's tail in our simultaneous delight in and despair of, for example, a perfect flying change. We experience a sense of ecstasy in the accomplishment, yet are sobered by the question of whether we can repeat it over and over and over in rapid succession.

The white stage is next, not to be confused with the earlier "whitening." In alchemic literature, to proceed to this stage meant one had attained a higher level of spiritual development. The white stage was often symbolized by a queen dressed in shining white robes. This stage marked the process of inner change by which the alchemist was able to experience and integrate the feminine component of the soul.

I remember a lesson with one of my male students who was struggling to master downward transitions — that is, the switch from one gait, such as a trot, down to a slower or easier gait, such as a walk. The more he tried to follow my instructions for dampening the stride, the more awkward his transitions became. Finally, I told him to forget about the biomechanics of the movement and to simply let feminine energy flow though him. "Visualize yourself as a beautiful sylph, Bill, astride a mythic unicorn," I said, and within moments Bill and his horse were transformed. The horse softened and the downward transitions flowed smoothly forward. In alchemic literature, the white stage was sometimes symbolized by the unicorn, because the unicorn could be tamed only by the touch of the purely feminine. When we ride the unicorn, we are confronted with our internal feminine forces. We begin to open the next developmental door as we resolve our feelings about these forces.

The next door is the reddening, and here we ride

an antlered stag. The reddening transforms the masculine forces of the soul: it ennobles them and brings them into a new harmony. I had a student who was chronically victimized by every horse she rode. Every horse she sat on sensed her uncertainty within seconds and seized control. Her horse would wander off the track, initiate unsolicited transitions, and stargaze out the arena door as she struggled to find her masculine essence. Finally, after an arduous confrontation with her inner self, she found her yang energy and rode the antlered stag. When the stag and the unicorn meet in the forest of our souls, they usher in the final stage of the journey.

The final stage is symbolized by the phoenix rising from the flames. In alchemical allegory, it marks the rebirth of personality in the crucible of transformation. As the alchemists sought to grasp both the inner parallels between each of the stages of the process, and the significance of each of the stages, they experienced inner death and rebirth. Once they found solid ground in the soul, they were able to creatively take hold of their lives and root their personalities in solid inner experience. When we ride the phoenix forward and upward out of the flames of the crucible, we become an *ecuyer*. Old things pass away, and everything else becomes new. This is the turning point in our journey. In contemporary psychological language, it could be said that we have initiated a transpersonal experience, that we have participated in the full spectrum of consciousness. From this place, we no longer merely look *in at* dressage, for now we see *out from* it.

CHAPTER 6

THE FOURTH DIMENSION

*He who sees the inaction that is in action and the action
that is in inaction is wise indeed.*

— **BHAGAVAD GITA**

It is not important — not really — that you ever learn to execute a flawless flying change. If you do, great! But, if you don't, humankind is no worse off. It is important, however, that you actualize your full human potential, for that does prosper humankind. It's unfortunate that contemporary competitive dressage evaluates an individual's experience primarily by means of test scores. This is an extremely reductionistic viewpoint that devalues the transformative potential of the art by confining it to what Ken Wilber calls flatland, a state of consciousness that is incomplete, disintegrated. The movements made by horse and rider are reduced to lines, circles, squares, and other figures that can be executed only on the surface of the manège, and that have no power to rise above or sink below it. From this perspective, the horse and rider's execution of the geometric movements is only physical and, therefore, three-dimensional. In contrast, new-paradigm thinking recognizes the sacred, or fourth-dimensional, potential in the art of dressage.

Author Rudy Rucker notes, "The fourth dimension is essentially a modern idea, dating back not much further than the mid-nineteenth century."[1] Although the vague notion of a higher reality has always been with us, the concept of a geometrical fourth dimension developed around 1840. According to Rucker, thought about the existence of a higher reality eventually led to a view of a fourth dimension that was "not only a spatial concept but a type of consciousness, an awareness of greater complexities and higher unities."[2] New-paradigm thinking suggests that the art of dressage could potentially supply sufficient creative energy to move a rider out of the strictly third-dimensional sphere of material existence to a higher dimension of existence, a fourth dimension of spirit. As Gene Savoy puts it, "Once inside this fourth-dimensional world, a person has access to a mirror image of the physical world. It is as if one is occupying two planes at the same time; the two figures are worlds apart, and yet they are within each other."[3]

An essential part of all art springs from the recognition of this creative unity in the human soul. According to Erich Neumann, "Primitive man regarded this creativity of the psyche as magic, and rightly so, for it transforms reality and will always do so."[4] At this creative-zero-point, consciousness and unconsciousness become momentarily unified, and the rider is joined with the unitary reality — in which there is no permanence, because all is transformation. Dressage aesthetics offer the "image and likeness of a primal creative force, prior to the world and outside the world, which," says Neumann, "though split from the very beginning into the polarity of nature and psyche, is in essence one undivided whole."[5] Via this creative solitude, an accomplished dressage artist escapes the prison of time and the limitations of ego-bound consciousness. What is manifest as the supreme alchemical transformation of the art is really a reflection of the alchemical transformation of the artist's personality.

If the alchemical transformation is fully experienced, the artist accepts that he or she is spirit, realizing his or her own immortality and, consequently, freedom. This path to liberation requires letting go of self and surrendering totally and unconditionally to the unitive power of love. "The ego is the dualist in us," says James P. Carse. "It is the habit we have of seeing ourselves over and against someone else."[6] From a liberated perspective, however, we see each opposing either-or as a conjoined either-or. We can be separate from our horse only because, at a deeper level, the horse and we are joined in something inseparable. According to Carse,

> *the still center, the soul, does not oppose anything. Not opposing anything, it does nothing. As soul, we do not act; we are. As ego, we cope with the world, change it, rearrange it, try to improve it. We cope with ourselves, too, becoming our own projects, struggling to be who and where we are not. When we become aware of the still-point in a person, of a deed that has no doer, we are aware of soul; we are in the presence of presence.*[7]

The dressage rider reaches the still center when he or she is no longer watching himself or herself, is neither thinking about riding nor being something outside of the horse.

It's significant that the word "animal" comes from the Latin *anima*, or "soul." Soul is not only the place of our still center but also the presence of the unutterable within us.[8] Horses are close to their own silence, close to the Tao. They let presence remain presence: unadulterated soul. As such, they can become the mirrors we cannot be to ourselves. If we pursue dressage technique to the exclusion of theory, we lose sight of the fact that knowledge rises from ignorance, thinking instead that it overcomes ignorance. Wild geese do not know where they are going, but they are not lost. "Knowledge can lift the veil," Carse points out. "It can also become the veil."[9] When we insist on rigid structure in our dressage practice, we struggle with our own spiritual sense of fluid self-transformation.

Our transformation is accelerated as our experience of the beautiful initiates an *ahimsa* experience. The Sanskrit word *ahimsa* means "dynamic compassion." This definition not only encompasses the renunciation of hurting any living being through hostile thought, word, or deed but also includes the conscious integration of compassion into every aspect of daily life.[10] We express ahimsa in our relationship with our horse when we serve as an active channel for compassion by opening our heart. The opening of our heart broadens our perceptual field, moving us beyond the limitations of three-dimensionality, so that we begin to see dressage in the fourth dimension.

Experiencing self-liberation while still in the physical body is one of the goals of people who have a three-dimensional understanding of reality. Once this is accomplished, one becomes aware of the four-dimensional archetypal forces operative in his or her life. Awareness of the archetypal consciousness stimulates our creative impulses. All great artists are adept at allowing archetypal intelligence into their minds and hearts.[11] The task is to open ourselves to, and consciously orchestrate, the reception of this energy. We can construct a model of the fourth dimension as a huge canopy of holographic film held over us, into which pour multidimensional layers of consciousness, manifest as waves of energy and light. Each dimensional layer, each beam of light, is something we can play with in ways that create a vision for overcoming the manifold dualities of third-dimensional existence.[12]

This vision of the fourth dimension allows waves of love to funnel through us, creating endless energy — an explosion of creative light — that affirms our unity with all that is.

ACKNOWLEDGMENTS

There is no way that I can adequately acknowledge all the people — and horses — who moved me toward writing *Dressage in the Fourth Dimension*. Sometimes it was simply a phrase that someone uttered, or the feel of a particular horse, that initiated the gestalts. Sufis say that, when the student is ready, the teacher will come . . . and this has certainly been the case in my life.

I am grateful to Egon von Neindorff and Henri van Schaik for their uncompromising efforts to help me get *inside* the art of dressage. I thank the four-legged professors, as well, who uncomplainingly let me practice until I was able to solve some of dressage's riddles. I remember, fondly, all the rectangular sand arenas that magically metamorphosed into cathedrals as I contemplated the dressage figures. Beth Hagens, an expert in the discipline of sacred geometry, was a source of constant encouragement, as was Peter Manchester, professor of ancient Greek philosophy. Robert Melik Finkle, artist extraordinaire, fueled the fires of my creative process, and fellow traveler Rufus Chafee pushed my inquiry to insight. Writer and artist Jane Pincus tirelessly read the early drafts in a collaborative process culminating in the production of her beautiful illustrations. The late Robert D. Davis was a veritable think tank who eagerly offered ideas and shared experiences. I gratefully acknowledge W. Charles Ballou, with whom I forged my preliminary vision for the book, as well as my daughter, Jec A. Ballou, who gave me a reason, during my dark night of the soul, to keep riding.

I thank my son, Pher Ballou, who taught me the meaning of steadfast friendship, and who remained curious about my interest in philosophy and dressage even as I, unintentionally, did not always reciprocate with the same zeal for his passions. And last, but in no way least, I make *gassho* to my life partner and best friend, Daniel A. Kealey, for supporting my passionate scholarship and never complaining about all the missed dinners, the horsehair covered sweaters, and the late nights that were the midwives to *Fourth Dimension*.

NOTES

INTRODUCTION

1. Aldous Huxley, *The Perennial Philosophy* (New York: Harper and Brothers, 1945)', vii.
2. Ibid.
3. Ibid.
4. Michele Cassou and Stewart Cubley, *Life, Paint, and Passion: Reclaiming the Magic of Spontaneous Expression*, foreword by Natalie Goldberg (New York: G. P. Putnam's Sons, 1995), xviii.
5. Ibid., xix.
6. Ibid., xx.

1. SACRED GEOMETRY

1. Robert Lawlor, *Sacred Geometry: Philosophy and Practice* (New York: Thames and Hudson, 1989), 6.
2. Charles de Kunffy, *The Ethics and Passions of Dressage* (Middletown, MD: Half Halt Press, 1993), 42.

3. Kenneth Sylvan Guthrie, *The Pythagorean Sourcebook and Library* (Grand Rapids, MI: Phanes Press, 1987), 321.

4. Iamblichus, *The Theology of Arithmetic*, translated by Robin Waterfield (Grand Rapids, MI: Phanes Press, 1988), 35–37.

5. De Kunffy, *Ethics*, 43–44.

6. A. T. Mann and Jane Lyle, *Sacred Sexuality* (New York: Barnes and Noble, 1995), 9.

7. For a good overview of Sperry's work, see Erika Erdmann and David Stover, *Beyond a World Divided: Human Values in the Brain-Mind Science of Roger Sperry* (Boston: Shambhala Publishing, 1991).

8. Gottfried Wilhelm Leibniz, *Discourse on Metaphysics* and *The Monadology*, edited by Albert R. Chandler, translated by George R. Montgomery (Mineola, NY: Dover Publications, 2005), 36.

9. Sri Aurobindo, *The Life Divine*, bk. 10, 3rd ed. (New York: India Library Society, 1965).

10. Lawlor, *Sacred Geometry*, 44–45.

11. Étienne Beudant, *Dressage du Cheval de Selle* [Training the Horse under Saddle] (1929; reprint, Paris: Réédition aux Éditions Jean-Michel Place, 1987), 27. A French cavalryman, Beudant (1861–1949) is considered one of the modern masters of dressage.

12. Lao Tzu, *Tao Te Ching*, translated by Stephen Mitchell (New York: Harper and Row, 1988), 48.

13. Michele Cassou and Stewart Cubley, *Life, Paint, and Passion: Reclaiming the Magic of Spontaneous Expression*, foreword by Natalie Goldberg (New York: G. P. Putnam's Sons, 1995), 2.

14. Iamblichus, *Theology*, 41.

15. Ibid.

16. Ibid., 55.

17. Ibid., 57.

18. François Robichon de la Guérinière, *École de Cavalerie* (Cleveland Heights, OH: Xenophon Press, 1992), 89.

2. TRANSCENDENTAL UNION

1. Indra Sinha, *The Great Book of Tantra* (Rochester, VT: Destiny Books, 1993), 109.

2. Robert Bly, James Hillman, and Michael Meade, eds., *The Rag and Bone Shop of the Heart* (New York: Harper Perennial, 1992), 3.

3. William Butler Yeats, "Mad as the Mist and Snow," in *The Winding Stair and Other Poems* (1933; reprint, Glacier National Park, MT: Kessinger Publishing, 2004), 21; Jung is quoted in Bly, Hillman, and Meade, eds., *The Rag and Bone Shop of the Heart*, 4.

4. Blake is quoted in Bly, Hillman, and Meade, eds., *The Rag and Bone Shop of the Heart*, 4.

5. Aldous Huxley, *The Perennial Philosophy* (New York: Harper and Brothers, 1945), 98.

6. Charles de Kunffy, *The Ethics and Passions of Dressage* (Middletown, MD: Half Halt Press, 1993), 46.

7. Sally Swift, *Centered Riding* (New York: St. Martin's Press, 1985), 17.

8. Paul Belasik, *Riding toward the Light: An Apprenticeship in the Art of Dressage Riding* (London: J. A. Allen & Co., 1990), 11.

3. RESPONSIBLE POWER

1. Mircea Eliade, *Yoga: Immortality and Freedom*, translated by Willard R. Trask (Princeton, NJ: Princeton University Press, 1958), 26.

2. Georg Feuerstein, trans., *The Yoga-Sutra of Patañjali* (Rochester, VT: Inner Traditions International, 1989), 11, 47. The Yoga Sutras of Patañjali come from an ancient, foundational yoga text and contain a whole range of meditation practices. You can find the sutras online at www.dailyreadings.com/sutras_1.htm.

3. Sally Swift has supplied images for the rider to visualize while riding that are designed to improve his or her postural alignment. The "spruce tree" guides the rider to sit up tall ("stretching his/her branches toward the sun") and keep the legs long ("stretching his/her roots down into the earth"), like a spruce tree. *Centered Riding* (New York: St. Martin's Press, 1985), 58.

4. Vasant G. Rele, *The Mysterious Kundalini* (Bombay: D.B. Taraporevala Sons, 1927), 6.

5. Swami Mukerji, *The Doctrine and Practice of Yoga* (Chicago: Yogi Publications Society, 1922), 11.

6. Plotinus (c. 204–270 CE) is widely considered to be the founder of Neoplatonism. Central to his philosophy is the idea that the entire hierarchy of spiritual reality exists within the individual human soul.

7. Dominique Barbier and Mary Daniels, *Dressage for the New Age* (New York: Prentice Hall, 1990), xi.

8. Robert Masters, *Neurospeak* (Wheaton, IL: Theosophical Publishing House, 1994), xii.

9. Chuck Grant (1914–1990) called himself the father of American dressage, though not everyone agreed with this assessment. Grant judged the first civilian (as opposed to military) dressage show held in the United States, in 1948, in Morton Grove, Illinois.

10. Jean-Claude Racinet, "Legerete vs. Durchlassigkeit" in *Dressage & CT* (May 1993): 11.

11. Aldous Huxley, *The Perennial Philosophy* (New York: Harper and Brothers, 1945), 219.

12. Evelyn Underhill, *Mysticism: A Study in the Nature and Development of Man's Spiritual Consciousness* (New York: E. P. Dutton, 1961), 333.

13. Pranab Bandyopadhyay, *The Goddess of Tantra* (Calcutta: Sankar Bhattacharya, 1990), 298.

14. Ibid., 298–99.

4. THE HYMN OF LOVE

1. Alla Renee Bozarth, *At the Foot of the Mountain* (Minneapolis: CompCare, 1990), 19.
2. Thomas Moore, *Soul Mates* (New York: HarperCollins, 1994), xv.
3. Bozarth, *At the Foot*, 32.
4. Flora B. Levin, *The Manual of Harmonics of Nicomachus the Pythagorean* (Grand Rapids, MI: Phanes Press, 1996), 16.
5. Charles de Kunffy, *Training Strategies for Dressage Riders* (Middletown, MD: Half Halt Press, 1996), 119.
6. According to Buber, human beings may adopt one of two attitudes toward other individuals in the world: they may see themselves as being in an I-Thou relationship with another or in an I-It relationship. I-Thou is a relationship of subject-to-subject, while I-It is a relationship of subject-to-object. In the I-Thou relationship, human beings do not perceive each other as consisting of specific, isolated qualities, and instead relate to each other as whole beings. In the I-It relationship, human beings perceive each other as consisting of specific, isolated qualities and view themselves as part of a world that consists of things. I-Thou is a relationship of mutuality and reciprocity, while I-It is a relationship of separateness and detachment. *I-Thou*, translated by Ronald Gregor Smith, 2nd ed. (New York: Charles Scribner's Sons, 1958).
7. Ibid., 132.

5. THE PATH OF THE SOUL

1. Plotinus, said to have been born in 204 or 205 CE, began his study of philosophy in his late twenties at Alexandria. In this cosmopolitan center of learning, Western and Eastern cultural influences coincided and a variety of philosophical schools flourished. Under the tutelage of Ammonius, Plotinus became well read in the works of Plato, Aristotle, and

their later commentators and became familiar with the writings of other major schools of philosophy, notably that of the Stoics.

In his thirty-ninth year, hoping to become acquainted with the philosophies of Persia and India, Plotinus joined a military campaign led by the emperor Gordian III (238–44 CE), which would prove disastrous. Upon the defeat of Gordian III, Plotinus escaped with difficulty and, later, settled in Rome, where he pursued the rest of his life's work. His philosophy is based on the premise that the individual human being is a microcosm of the universe. The true self, identified with the rational soul, is akin to the great Soul of the World, the Logos that creates and orders the visible universe and organizes all the emanations of the One, all the parts of the material world. Just as reason in the individual is informed by truths self-evident to intellect, by the highest activity of mind, so the Soul of the World eternally contemplates the intelligible forms that represent the thoughts of the universal intelligence. The material universe, like the human body, is a faded image of the One and a thing of temporal process: reality, or true being, consists of states of consciousness arranged within a hierarchy of spiritual activity, and is eternal.

At the center of an individual soul, a person can attain union with the Infinite Principle of all creation, that which engenders all of existence, and to which all that exists longs to revert. The Infinite Principle, as absolute and self-sufficient simplicity, is called the One, and also, as the goal to which all things aspire, the good. It may also be called power, will, beauty, and/or love. (My discussion of Plotinus in this book draws on his volume *The Enneads III: Abridged Edition*, edited by John Dillon, translated by Stephen MacKenna (New York: Penguin Classics, 1991).

2. Ibid., sec. 9.
3. Ibid., sec. 16.
4. George Leonard, *Mastery* (New York: Dutton, 1991), 140.

5. Ken Wilber, "The Way Up Is the Way Down," *Parabola* 20, no. 4 (Winter 1995): 86.

6. Ibid.

7. Alchemy in its highest aspect deals with the spiritual regeneration of humankind and teaches how a god may be made out of a human being — that is, how to establish the conditions necessary for the development of divine powers in human beings, so that a human may became a god by the power of God, in the same sense that a seed becomes a plant by the aid of the four elements and the action of the invisible fifth element, the life force. My discussion of alchemy in the chapter and this note draws on Adam McLean's *A Commentary on the Mutus Liber* (Grand Rapids, MI: Phanes Press, 1991).

6. THE FOURTH DIMENSION

1. Rudy Rucker, *The Fourth Dimension: Toward a Geometry of Higher Reality* (Boston: Houghton Mifflin, 1984), 58.

2. Ibid., 59.

3. Gene Savoy, *Project X: The Search for the Secrets of Immortality* (Indianapolis: Bobbs-Merill, 1977), 117.

4. Erich Neumann, *Art and the Creative Unconscious* (Princeton, NJ: Princeton University Press, 1971), 203.

5. Ibid., 103.

6. James P. Carse, *Breakfast at the Victory: The Mysticism of Ordinary Experience* (San Francisco: HarperCollins, 1995), 11.

7. Ibid., 12.

8. Ibid., 21.

9. Ibid., 30.

10. Nathaniel Altman, *Ahimsa: Dynamic Compassion* (Wheaton, IL: Theosophical Publishing House, 1980), 5.

11. Barbara Hand Clow, *The Pleiadian Agenda: A New Cosmology for the Age of Light* (Santa Fe, NM: Bear and Co., 1995), 131.

12. Ibid., 132.

BIBLIOGRAPHY

Altman, Nathaniel. *Ahimsa: Dynamic Compassion*. Wheaton, IL: Theosophical Publishing House, 1980.

Armstrong, Arthur Hilary, ed. *The Cambridge History of Later Greek and Early Medieval Philosophy*. Cambridge: Cambridge University Press, 1967.

———, ed. *Classical Mediterranean Spirituality*. Vol. 15 of *World Spirituality*, ed. Ewert Cousins. New York: Crossroad Publishing, 1986.

———. *Hellenic and Christian Studies*. Brookfield, VT: Gower Publishers, 1990.

Ashvaghosha. *The Awakening of Faith*. Translated by D. T. Suzuki. Chicago: Open Court Publishing, 1990.

Aurobindo, S. *The Life Divine*. Bk. 10. 3rd ed. New York: India Library Society, 1965.

———. *The Synthesis of Yoga*. Pondicherry, India: Aurobindo Ashram Press, 1957.

———. *On Yoga II*. Pondicherry, India: Aurobindo Ashram Press, 1958.

Bandyopadhyay, Pranab. *The Goddess of Tantra*. Calcutta: Sankar Bhattacharya, 1990.

Barbier, Dominique, and Mary Daniels. *Dressage for the New Age*. New York: Prentice Hall, 1990.

Basu, Durga Das. *The Essence of Hinduism*. New Delhi: Prentice Hall of India, 1990.

Belasik, Paul. *Riding toward the Light: An Apprenticeship in the Art of Dressage Riding*. London: J. A. Allen & Co., 1990.

Berry, Thomas. *The Dream of the Earth*. San Francisco: Sierra Club, 1988.

Beudant, Étienne. *Dressage du Cheval de Selle*. 1929. Reprint, Paris: Réédition aux Éditions Jean-Michel Place, 1987.

Birch, C., and J. B. Cobb Jr. *The Liberation of Life*. Cambridge: Cambridge University Press, 1981.

Blake, Henry. *Talking with Horses: A Study of Communication between Man and Horse*. North Pomfret, VT: Trafalgar Square Publishing, 1975.

Bly, Robert, James Hillman, and Michael Meade, eds. *The Rag and Bone Shop of the Heart*. New York: Harper Perennial, 1992.

Bohm, David. *Wholeness and the Implicate Order*. London: Routledge and Kegan Paul, 1980.

Bozarth, Alla Renee. *At the Foot of the Mountain*. Minneapolis, MN: CompCare, 1990.

Buber, Martin. *I-Thou*. Translated by Ronald Gregor Smith. 2nd ed. New York: Charles Scribner's Sons, 1958.

Burke, James. *The Day the Universe Changed*. Boston: Little, Brown, 1985.

Carse, James P. *Breakfast at the Victory: The Mysticism of Ordinary Experience*. San Francisco: HarperCollins, 1995.

Cassou, Michele, and Stewart Cubley. *Life, Paint, and Passion: Reclaiming the Magic of Spontaneous Expression*. Foreword by Natalie Goldberg. New York: G. P. Putnam's Sons, 1995.

Clow, Barbara Hand. *The Pleiadian Agenda: A New Cosmology for the Age of Light*. Santa Fe, NM: Bear & Co, 1995.

Day, Harvey. *About Yoga: The Complete Philosophy*. New York: British Book Centre, 1951.

Decarpentry, General. *Academic Equitation*. London: J. A. Allen & Co., 1971.

de Kunffy, Charles. *The Ethics and Passions of Dressage*. Middletown, MD: Half Halt Press, 1993.

————. *Training Strategies for Dressage Riders*. Middletown, MD: Half Halt Press, 1996.

de la Guérinière, Francois Robichon. *École de Cavalerie*. Cleveland Heights, OH: Xenophon Press, 1992.

Eliade, Mircea. *Yoga: Immortality and Freedom*. Translated by Willard R. Trask. Princeton, NJ: Princeton University Press, 1958.

Erdman, Erika, and David Stover. *Beyond a World Divided: Human Values in the Brain-Mind Science of Roger Sperry*. Boston: Shambhala Publishing, 1991.

Faivre, Antoine. *Access to Western Esotericism*. Albany: State University of New York Press, 1994.

Fernando, Ranjit, ed. *The Unanimous Tradition: Essays on the Essential Unity of all Religions*. Colombo: Sri Lanka Institute of Traditional Studies, 1991.

Feuerstein, Georg, trans. *The Yoga-Sutra of Patañjali*. Rochester, VT: Inner Traditions International, 1989.

Froissard, Jean. *Classical Horsemanship for Our Time*. Gaithersburg, MD: Half Halt Press, 1988.

Guthrie, Kenneth Sylvan. *The Pythagorean Sourcebook and Library*. Grand Rapids, MI: Phanes Press, 1987.

Hassler, Jill Keiser. *Beyond the Mirrors: The Study of the Mental and Spiritual Aspects of Horsemanship*. Quarryville, PA: Goals Unlimited Press, 1988.

Hayward, Jeremy. *Shifting Worlds, Changing Minds: Where the Sciences and Buddhism Meet*. Boston: Shambhala Publishing, 1987.

Herbermann, Erik F. *The Dressage Formula*. London: J. A. Allen & Co., 1980.

Huxley, Aldous. *The Perennial Philosophy*. New York: Harper and Brothers, 1945.

Iamblichus. *The Theology of Arithmetic*. Translated by Robin Waterfield. Grand Rapids, MI: Phanes Press, 1988.

Inge, William Ralph. *The Philosophy of Plotinus*. New York: Greenwood Press, 1968.

Jousseaume, Andre. *Progressive Dressage*. London: J.A. Allen & Co., 1978.

Lao Tzu. *Tao Te Ching*. Translated by Stephen Mitchell. New York: Harper and Row, 1988.

Laszlo, Ervin. *The Self-Organizing Universe*. Oxford: Pergamon Press, 1980.

Lawlor, Robert. *Sacred Geometry: Philosophy and Practice*. New York: Thames and Hudson, 1989.

Leibniz, Gottfried Wilhelm. *Discourse on Metaphysics* and *The Monadology*. Edited by Albert R. Chandler. Translated by George R. Montgomery. Mineola, NY: Dover Publications, 2005.

Leonard, George. *Mastery*. New York: Dutton Books, 1991.

Levin, Flora A. *The Manual of Harmonics of Nicomachus the Pythagorean*. Grand Rapids, MI: Phanes Press, 1994.

Loch, Sylvia. *The Classical Seat*. London: Unwin Hyman, 1988.

Mann, A.T., and Jane Lyle. *Sacred Sexuality*. New York: Barnes and Noble, 1995.

Masih, Yakub. *The Classical Religious Philosophy of the Hindus*. Patna, India: Kasji Prasad Jayaswal Research Institute, 1991.

Masters, Robert. *Neurospeak*. Wheaton, IL: Theosophical Publishing House, 1994.

Mather, H.S. *The Science of Awakening Consciousness: Our Ancient Wisdom*. New Delhi: Occult India Publications, 1990.

McElroy, Susan Chernak. *Animals as Teachers and Healers*. Troutdale, OR: New Sage Press, 1996.

McLean, Adam. *A Commentary on the Mutus Liber*. Grand Rapids, MI: Phanes Press, 1991.

Moore, Thomas. *Soul Mates*. New York: HarperCollins, 1994.

Mukerji, Swami. *The Doctrine and Practice of Yoga*. Chicago: Yogi Publications Society, 1922.

Nasr, Seyyed Hossein. *Knowledge and the Sacred*. Albany: State University of New York Press, 1989.

Neumann, Erich. *Art and the Creative Unconscious*. Translated by Ralph Manheim. Princeton, NJ: Princeton University Press, 1971.

Nie, Hua Ching. *The Quest of the Soul*. Malibu, CA: Shrine of the Eternal Breath of the Tao; Los Angeles: College of Tao and Traditional Chinese Healing, 1989.

———. *Tao: The Subtle Universal Law and the Integral Way of Life*. 2nd ed. Santa Monica, CA: Sevenstar Communications, 1993.

Oliveira, Nuno. *Horses and Their Riders*. Wamambool, Australia: Howley and Russell, 1988.

———. *Reflections on Equestrian Art*. Translated by Phyllis Field. London: J. A. Allen & Co., 1976.

Ornstein, Robert. *The Evolution of Consciousness*. New York: Prentice Hall, 1991.

Ornstein, Robert, and Paul Ehrlich. *New World, New Mind*. New York: Simon and Schuster, 1990.

Ouspensky, P. D. *In Search of the Miraculous*. San Diego, CA: Harcourt Brace Jovanovich, 1949.

Peat, F. David. *Synchronicity: The Bridge between Mind and Matter*. New York: Bantam, 1987.

Petushkova, Yelena. *My Life and My Dressage Horses*. Translated by Vivienne Burdon. Moscow: Raduga Publishers, 1983.

Plotinus. *The Enneads III: Abridged Edition*. Edited by John Dillon. Translated by Stephen MacKenna. New York: Penguin Classics, 1991.

Podhajsky, Alois. *My Horses, My Teachers*. Elverson, PA: Bright Books, 1987.

Powers, Suzanne. *He Dared to Love a Horse: A Treatise on Dressage Equitation*. Chagrin Falls, OH: privately printed, 1987.

Prasad, N. S. *Convergence of Science and Hindu Philosophy*. Delhi: Motilal Banarsidass, 1989.

Racinet, Jean-Claude. *Another Horsemanship*. Cleveland Heights, OH: Xenophon Press, 1994.

———. "Legerete vs. Durchlassigkeit." *Dressage & CT* (May 1993).

Rele, Vasant G. *The Mysterious Kundalini*. Bombay: D. B. Taraporevala Sons, 1927.

Roney-Dougal, Serena. *Where Science and Magic Meet*. Shaftsbury, England: Element Books, 1991.

Rucker, Rudy. *The Fourth Dimension: Toward a Geometry of Higher Reality*. Boston: Houghton Mifflin, 1984.

Savoy, Gene. *Project X: The Search for the Secrets of Immortality*. Indianapolis: Bobbs-Merrill, 1977.

Schuon, F. *The Transcendent Unity of Religions*. New York: Harper and Row, 1976.

Sharpe, Kevin. *David Bohm's World: New Physics and New Religion*. Levisburg, PA: Bucknell University Press, 1993.

Shaw, Gregory. *Theurgy and the Soul: The Neoplatonism of Iamblichus*. University Park: Pennsylvania State University Press, 1995.

Sinha, Indra. *The Great Book of Tantra*. Rochester, VT: Destiny Books, 1993.

Stevens, Jose, and Simon Warwick-Smith. *The Michael Handbook: A Channeled System for Self-Understanding*. Sonoma, CA: Warwick Press, 1990.

Swift, Sally. *Centered Riding*. New York: St. Martin's Press, 1985.

Talbot, Michael. *The Holographic Universe*. New York: HarperCollins, 1991.

Three Initiates. *The Kybalion: The Hermetic Philosophy of Ancient Egypt and Greece*. Clayton, GA: Tri-State Press, 1988.

Underhill, Evelyn. *Mysticism: A Study in the Nature and Development of Man's Spiritual Consciousness*. New York: E. P. Dutton, 1961.

van Schaik, H. L. M. *Misconceptions and Simple Truths in Dressage.* London: J. A. Allen & Co., 1986.

Walsch, Neale Donald. *Conversations with God: An Uncommon Dialogue.* Charlottesville, VA: Hampton Roads Publishing, 1995.

Wilber, Ken. *The Atman Project: A Transpersonal View of Human Development.* Wheaton, IL: Theosophical Publishing House, 1980.

————. *Eye to Eye: The Quest for the New Paradigm.* Boston: Shambhala Publishing, 1990.

————. *No Boundary: Eastern and Western Approaches to Personal Growth.* Boston: Shambhala Publishing, 1981.

————. *Sex, Ecology, and Spirituality.* Boston: Shambhala Publishing, 1995.

————. "The Way Up Is the Way Down." *Parabola* 20, no. 4 (Winter 1995): 65–71.

Xenophon. *The Principles of Horsemanship.* Translated by M. H. Morgan. London: J. A. Allen & Co., 1984.

INDEX

ABOUT THE AUTHOR

Sherry L. Ackerman, PhD, is a professor of philosophy at the College of the Siskiyous, in Weed, California, as well as an internationally acclaimed dressage clinician. She sees dressage as transformational, as an avenue to reflection, exploration, and self-knowledge through which riders can experience liberation from their narrowly individual, egoistic I-ness. Ackerman is one of the American dressage industry's leading proponents of dressage as a philosophical, spiritual, and artistic practice.

Dressage in the Fourth Dimension has been a pioneer work in awakening dressage consciousness, a finger pointing at the moon. Now in its second edition, its message is right on time. It requires readers to deconstruct every assumption they have ever held, to ask "Why?" and become okay with not-knowing.

Humanity's alienation from nature can no longer be ignored. The enormity and immediacy of the crisis is evident. Dr. Ackerman's work during the last few years has been concerned with the theme of liberation. She points readers toward a consideration of humanity's liberation from societal conditioning, from externally legislated morality and normative thinking, and ultimately, from the egoistic self. She believes that getting beyond one's own ideas, and discovering the context of one's own thinking, is liberating. Identifying the differences between what we think that we think, and the conditioned, enculturated patterns of thought handed down to us, opens interesting avenues for growth and transformation. Dr. Ackerman's concept of the fourth dimension requires readers to leave the analytic, objective mind behind and enter into the mystery of inspiration.

Dr. Ackerman lives at the foot of Mount Shasta, in California, and attempts in the silence of the woods to practice what *Dressage in the Fourth Dimension* teaches. Living quietly with her horses, she seeks transformation.

For more information, see
www.sherryackerman.com.